THE BLENDED COURSE DESIGN
WORKBOOK

THE BLENDED COURSE DESIGN WORKBOOK

A Practical Guide

Kathryn E. Linder

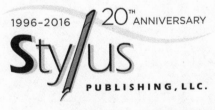

1996–2016 20TH ANNIVERSARY

Stylus PUBLISHING, LLC.

STERLING, VIRGINIA

COPYRIGHT © 2017 BY
STYLUS PUBLISHING, LLC.

Published by Stylus Publishing, LLC.
22883 Quicksilver Drive
Sterling, Virginia 20166-2102

Library of Congress Cataloging-in-Publication Data
Names: Linder, Kathryn E.
Title: The blended course design workbook : a practical guide /
Kathryn E. Linder.
Description: Sterling, Virginia : Stylus Publishing, 2016. |
Includes bibliographical references and index.
Identifiers: LCCN 2016014459|
  ISBN 9781620364352 (cloth : alk. paper) |
  ISBN 9781620364369 (pbk. : alk. paper) |
  ISBN 9781620364376 (library networkable e-edition) |
  ISBN 9781620364383 (consumer e-edition)
Subjects: LCSH: Blended learning. |
Instructional systems--Design.
Classification: LCC LB1028.5 .L56 2016 |
DDC 371.3--dc23
LC record available at https://lccn.loc.gov/2016014459

13-digit ISBN: 978-1-62036-435-2 (cloth)
13-digit ISBN: 978-1-62036-436-9 (paperback)
13-digit ISBN: 978-1-62036-437-6 (library networkable e-edition)
13-digit ISBN: 978-1-62036-438-3 (consumer e-edition)

Printed in the United States of America

All first editions printed on acid-free paper
that meets the American National Standards Institute
Z39-48 Standard.

Bulk Purchases

Quantity discounts are available for use in workshops and for
staff development.
Call 1-800-232-0223

First Edition, 2017

10   9   8   7   6   5

For Brenda Hardin, who raised me to be resilient;

For Pam Corpron Parker, who raised me as a writer
and who helped me to see the value of hard work;

And for Judy Winter, who raised my partner
and who consistently models what it means to be a true lifelong learner.

CONTENTS

TABLES, FIGURES, AND BOXES

FIGURES

BOXES

ACKNOWLEDGMENTS

This book, more than anything else I have written, was dependent on the insights, suggestions, and feedback of trusted colleagues. I offer my appreciation to my coauthors, who shared their expertise and experience to help make this book as practical as possible. Victoria, Sarah, Danny, and Linda, I had so much fun writing with and learning from each of you! I also want to offer my thanks to the three anonymous reviewers who offered many thoughtful suggestions on an earlier draft. This would not be the same book without those reviewers' contributions and I thank them for their time and attention to detail.

The seed for this book was planted because of a faculty development program, the Hybrid Course Design Institute (HCDI), which was codesigned and cofacilitated while I worked at the Center for Teaching and Scholarly Excellence (CTSE) at Suffolk University. The HCDI was created at the request of Suffolk's former president, Jim McCarthy, who came to Suffolk with the idea to launch a hybrid teaching initiative; many thanks to Jim for encouraging me to learn more about the blended modality and the benefits it can offer for students and instructors. I also offer a huge thank-you to all of the Suffolk University faculty members and administrators who participated in the HCDI and offered feedback on what worked best for them when designing blended courses. I extend a special thank you to those faculty members who shared examples and resources for this book; Pat Hogan, Eric Dewar, Alison Kelly, and Margarita DiVall, you helped me make the abstract more concrete. I also want to thank two former CTSE staff members who helped develop the HCDI program, Sarah Smith and Danny Fontaine (also coauthors of this book), and Linda Bruenjes (also a coauthor) and Rebecca Sullivan who also worked with me at Suffolk University in the CTSE. Each of these colleagues offered unparalleled support as I worked on this book project. The bulk of this book was written while I worked at Suffolk University, so I also extend my appreciation to Jeff Pokorak, my boss at the time, who completely supported the writing and publication of this project. Members of the Suffolk University faculty writing group were also a huge support for me—thanks to all of you who shared your writing struggles and accomplishments and encouraged me along the way.

Another key contributor to this project, Kirsten Behling, generously provided the accessibility rubric found in Chapter 14. I also extend much appreciation to Kirsten for the friendship and emotional support she provided during the writing of this book—frequent check-ins on the status of the draft kept me on task!

I could not have written this book without the knowledge and training I gained in course and curriculum design from my colleagues at the University Center for the Advancement of Teaching (UCAT) at The Ohio State University—thank you to all my UCAT colleagues for sharing their expertise and encouraging me to build on it.

I also want to extend my thanks to my current colleagues at Oregon State University Extended Campus for the support and excitement they share regarding my writing projects.

I have been incredibly fortunate to work with the dedicated team at Stylus Publishing. A special thanks to David Brightman and Alex Hartnett for ushering this book through the various stages of review and revision toward publication; I've appreciated your insights and support, and I am so glad that we have gotten the chance to work together.

Thanks to my family for supporting the long haul of another book project. To Mom and Craig, Ralph and Judy, Beth and Matt, Sarah, Megan and Brett, my five nieces and nephews, and my Gram and Grandpa, many thanks for asking about the status of the book and offering your support during the drafting and revision process.

And, finally, there are practically no words to describe my appreciation for Ben, who put up with writing binges, revision anxieties, extensive conversations about blended teaching and learning, and a frequently distracted partner during this process. Ben, I truly could not have done it without you—my deepest thanks and love for your unwavering support and unparalleled confidence in my abilities.

INTRODUCTION

Why Blended, Why Now?

Over the past several decades, a wide range of technologies has emerged that are designed to assist in teaching and learning. Technology has changed every aspect of our lives, and the higher education classroom also feels that impact (Collins & Halverson, 2009). Distance education programs at institutions of higher education, which are often seen as a means to broaden enrollment and increase gross margins (e.g., see Parry, 2011), are continuing to grow (Allen & Seaman, 2014). Blended (also referred to as hybrid) courses, in which face-to-face interaction is combined with technology-enhanced or online activities to aid student learning, have also been posed as a possible solution to the question of how best to engage busy students in a cost-effective and learner-centered way. Major (2015) points out that, for some, blended is seen to be "the best of both worlds" (p. 82) because of the way it allows for both face-to-face interaction and online support structures. For many instructors across disciplines, a form of blended learning, termed *flipped classrooms*, has also gained popularity as a method to increase in-class active learning time by shifting delivery of content to the online environment.

Since their inception, blended teaching and learning environments have been explored from a range of perspectives. In this workbook, I want to start by offering an overview of the research on blended environments by answering the following key questions:

1. What is blended teaching and learning?
2. What do we know about the effectiveness of blended platforms, tools, strategies, and techniques?
3. How do we know that blended learning is effective?
4. For whom are blended learning environments effective?

Following this review of the research, the chapter will end with an explanation of how this workbook is organized as well as suggestions for how to best use it. (In addition to this initial research overview, important theories, studies, and principles for blended course design are also referenced in each chapter throughout the workbook.)

What Is Blended Teaching and Learning?

Definitions of *blended teaching and learning* can vary, so it is important to establish what blended environments mean for the purpose of this workbook. Allen and

TABLE I.1.
Definitions of *Face-to-Face* Versus *Online Components*

Traditional	*Web-facilitated*	*Blended*	*Online*
0% content delivered online	1%–29% content delivered online	30%–79% content delivered online	80% or more content delivered online

Seaman (2007) offer helpful and concrete definitions for *face-to-face* versus *online components* in traditional, web-facilitated, blended, and online courses (see Table I.1).

Most definitions of *blended environments* agree on the following:

- A combination of face-to-face and online components make up the blended classroom environment (Garrison & Vaughan, 2008; Glazer, 2012; Picciano, 2007, 2009; Snart, 2010); and
- Students in the blended environment experience more self-directed, independent, and autonomous learning (Caulfield, 2011; Glazer, 2012).

Additionally, the following components are often cited for *effective* blended environments:

- Instructors intentionally choose technologies that support the course learning objectives (Picciano, 2009);
- Instructors purposely align face-to-face and online components for effective student learning (Glazer, 2012; Picciano, 2009); and
- Instructors deliberately embed active learning techniques and methodologies in the blended course (Caulfield, 2011; Glazer 2012).

Definitions of *blended environments* can disagree on the following:

- The ratio of face-to-face versus online time that comprises a blended course; and
- Whether a blended course must include online components designed to replace face-to-face instruction.

While some might argue that any time substantial technology is added into a course it becomes blended as long as the course is not completely held online, the majority of scholars agree that a course needs to have face-to-face time replaced by online content before it can be considered a truly blended course (Caulfield, 2011; Garrison & Vaughan, 2008; Glazer, 2012; Laster, Otte, Picciano, & Sorg, 2005). For example, a course that traditionally meets twice per week, when transitioned to a blended model with additional online content and components, might only meet face-to-face once per week. In this workbook, I do not specify a percentage of online engagement as part of the *blended* definition, but I do assume the replacement of face-to-face time as part of what comprises a blended modality. I also agree with Picciano's (2009) definition of *blended learning* as "courses that integrate online with traditional face-to-face class activities in a planned, pedagogically valuable manner" (p. 8). In other words, this workbook will demonstrate that a blended course, particularly one that is effective, does not happen by accident. Like any successful course, the blended modality requires intentional design components to ensure a well-structured learning environment.

What Do We Know About the Effectiveness of Blended Platforms, Tools, Strategies, and Techniques?

Several meta-analyses have been conducted to assess the effectiveness of online learning, including in blended environments; however, scholars generally agree that more empirical research on the blended modality is needed (e.g., see Picciano & Dziuban, 2007; Picciano, Dziuban, & Graham, 2014). The U.S. Department of Education (2010) found in an analysis of research from 1996 to 2008 that "on average, students in online learning conditions performed better than those receiving face-to-face instruction" (p. ix). The same study found that this was particularly true for blended environments, but noted that this may be because blended modalities include "additional learning time and instructional elements not received by students in control groups" (p. ix). However, a different meta-analysis of blended and online learning research by Lack (2013) found that "most of the studies have mixed results. . . . On some measures the online- or hybrid-format students did significantly better or worse than the students in the face-to-face format, but on other measures there was no significant difference between the two groups" (p. 11). In other words, the impacts of blended and online learning methods on student learning outcomes are not entirely definitive when measured through rigorous research (see Table I.2).

TABLE I.2.
Impacts of Blended and Online Learning Methods on Student Learning Outcomes

Findings	*Studies*
Better outcomes in blended learning environment	Du, 2011; Christou, Dinov, & Sanchez, 2007; Riffell & Sibley, 2005
Little to no difference between blended and online learning or face-to-face learning	Chen & Jones, 2007; Odell, Abbitt, Amos, & Davis, 1999; Reasons, Valdares, & Slavkin, 2005; Scoville & Buskirk, 2007; McNamara, Swalm, Stearne, & Covassin, 2008

Additional studies have attempted to measure particular components of the blended environment. For example, Borup, West, and Graham (2013) studied the impacts of asynchronous videos and Hall and Davison (2007) explored the use of blogs in blended environments. The literature on different components of blended teaching and learning continues to grow as instructors experiment with the modality, tools, and techniques. Ongoing research will provide additional evidence of the benefits or drawbacks of blended environments.

How Do We Know That Blended Learning Is Effective?

Because investigations of the effectiveness of blended environments are conducted "for the most part by professors and other instructors who are conducting research using their own courses" (U.S. Department of Education, 2010, p. 49), a range of data is collected and analyzed. Different forms of data might include pre- and posttests, final course grades, exam scores, quiz scores, paper or project grades, scores on homework assignments, completion rates, pass rates, course participation scores, withdrawal rates, and other measures. Use of a Learning Management System (LMS) allows for the collection of "analytics" regarding student participation in online components such as discussion boards, whether students watch videos, how long students spend on the LMS website, and other pieces of information. Unfortunately, much of analytics data can be quite "noisy" and difficult to interpret. For example, knowing that a student watched a video all the way through does not guarantee that the student was paying attention, taking notes, or thinking critically about the material presented.

Moreover, in their meta-analysis of research on the effectiveness of blended and online learning methods, the U.S. Department of Education (2010) cautions, "the combinations of technology, content, and activities used in different experimental conditions have often been ad hoc rather than theory based. As a result, the field lacks a coherent body of linked studies that systematically test theory-based approaches in different contexts" (p. 49). In her later meta-analysis, Lack (2013) also describes several challenges of conducting "rigorous research on educational outcomes, especially where human subjects and Institutional Review Board requirements are involved" and cites "barriers to randomization" and "implementing proper research protocols" (p. 13) as particular difficulties.

Given the increase in both blended and fully online courses and programs, the landscape of higher education as well as online education research is constantly changing. Blended and online learning are being hailed as part of the "disruptive innovation" (Christensen, 2011) currently being experienced in higher education; indeed, some consider blended courses to have "transformative potential" (Garrison & Kanuka, 2004, p. 95). Scholars have just begun to explore topics such as the institutional adoption and implementation of blended learning in higher education (Garrison & Vaughan, 2008; Graham, Woodfield, & Harrison, 2013), best practices for blended course design (Hensley, 2005; McGee & Reis, 2012), and questions of faculty load and the increased time needed for blended course design (Tynan, Ryan, & Lamont-Mills, 2015). As more blended courses and programs are developed, it will be important to expand the literature on course and program evaluation, structures and infrastructures to support blended environments, student persistence and retention in blended courses, cost containment and sustainability, and how to iterate and innovate blended courses to meet the needs of an ever-changing and diverse student population.

For Whom Are Blended Environments Effective?

The range of results in the studies cited previously in this chapter may be indicative of the diverse range of students taking blended and online courses in higher education. In relation to blended learning success, questions have been raised about different populations of students: (a) first-year students and first-generation students, (b) students with disabilities (SWD), and (c) students with varying degrees of motivation and engagement. Additional research on each of these populations will contribute to a better understanding of how well they can succeed in blended learning environments.

First-Year Students and First-Generation Students

There has been some concern that blended learning environments may ask too much of first-year students or first-generation students who are just learning how to succeed in a college environment. Because blended environments necessarily involve more self-directed learning, time-management skills, and more autonomy, some have questioned whether blended courses should even be an option for a first-year curriculum. However, initial studies have indicated that blended courses can offer a helpful transition for students (Moore & Gilmartin, 2010), especially for those who may already be using technology for learning in their high-school classrooms. Readiness quizzes, which can help students ascertain if they are prepared to succeed in a blended environment, can educate students about the kinds of additional challenges that are included in the blended environment as well as alert instructors to the range of experiences students have with technology use and autonomous learning environments (descriptions of these assessment tools can be found in Dray et al., 2011; Hung, Chou, Chen, & Own, 2010; and Pillay, Irving, & Tones, 2007). Introducing students to blended learning environments early in their college career may benefit them later on, particularly for institutions where blended courses comprise a large portion of the curriculum.

Students With Disabilities (SWD)

The flexibility available to students in blended environments can make blended courses an ideal place for embedding differentiated instruction that offers custom-designed learning activities for diverse student groups. Based on the principles of

Universal Design for Learning (UDL), differentiated instruction offers flexibility for instructors as they consider students' learning preferences, past experiences with the course content, and students' current interests (Burgstahler, 2008). Given that the application of UDL principles to more traditional learning environments has been tied to increased student engagement (Moore & Fetzner, 2009), persistence (Field, Sarver, & Shaw, 2003; Getzel, 2008), and retention (Field et al., 2003; Getzel, 2008; Moore & Fetzner, 2009), additional research on UDL in blended environments is needed to assess how the blended modality might impact the learning of SWDs. Although preliminary research has found that, for example, deaf or hard-of-hearing students may benefit from the blended environment (Starenko, Vignare, & Humbert, 2007), this research is not conclusive.

Students With Varying Degrees of Motivation and Engagment

Because blended learning environments depend on students to be self-directed and independent learners, there has been some concern that students must be especially motivated and engaged to succeed in a blended classroom. The combination of self-directed learning components with the intentional alignment between out-of-class and in-class components in a blended course means that a student can fall behind rather quickly by missing a face-to-face session or skipping homework. This is particularly true for students who enroll in a blended course expecting it to be easier than a traditional face-to-face environment. Given that Scholarship of Teaching and Learning (SoTL) scholars have pointed to the importance of motivation and engagement, more generally, for the success of all learners (e.g., see Ambrose et al., 2010; Svinicki, 2004), it is not surprising that these factors would also be of significance in the blended environment.

More research is certainly needed to measure whether blended environments more generally, as well as smaller components included in blended classrooms (tools, technologies, techniques), are effective for helping students learn. Until additional research is conducted, rigorously designed research can provide helpful information for instructors looking to develop best practices for blended course design. Moreover, blended instructors can look to already-existing best practice literature on aspects such as course design, active learning, and student engagement to guide the construction and implementation of a blended course. As Shea (2007) argues, "a key to ensuring the instructional quality of blended learning is to attend to what we know about quality learning environments generally, to keep in mind what we know about adult learners, and to integrate our burgeoning knowledge of online learning processes" (p. 28). This workbook integrates all three of these components to ensure the design of effective blended courses.

Organization of *The Blended Course Design Workbook*

The literature review in this chapter points to some of the challenges of blended classrooms for institutions of higher education. Here are a few that are pertinent to this workbook: (a) providing successful training to support faculty integration of technology into their pedagogy to enhance student learning, (b) creating support structures to acculturate students to more independent and self-directed learning environments, and (c) creating a technology support infrastructure for both instructors and students as the use of technology tools both inside and outside of class increases. To help address these challenges, this workbook provides a systematic training mechanism for faculty members interested in converting a traditional course to a blended model, discusses the needs of students as they begin to transition to more technology-mediated learning environments, and provides additional resources on institutional infrastructure best practices to ensure the successful implementation of blended courses and programs.

For faculty members, finding the time to transition a course to a blended format can be a huge challenge. Blended course design often necessitates a complete redesign of a traditional course to make sure that the technology tools are integrated as seamlessly as possible. The time needed to learn about the tools, reconfigure a course, redesign the LMS, and complete other necessary tasks such as the creation of course content modules or videos can seem overwhelming. This workbook was designed to help faculty members take on blended course design tasks in manageable pieces and through a systematic and comprehensive process.

For many students, blended environments present new challenges, particularly in time management and motivation. Throughout this workbook, we offer tested techniques to help students succeed in the blended classroom environment. Course design best practice always places the students and their learning at the center of the instructor's decision-making as the instructor drafts goals and objectives, plans learning activities and assessments, and maps out a course and its content week-by-week. This workbook will help course designers take students learning into account at every stage of the blended course design and construction process.

How to Use This Workbook

This workbook is specifically designed for instructors who are comfortable with classroom technologies as well as those who are just beginning to explore incorporating technology into their teaching. I believe that any instructor who has a passion for helping students learn can achieve success in the blended classroom. Thus, I welcome readers who come to blended learning with limited technology literacy or advanced experience with technology tools. I also believe that this workbook can provide tools and resources for more experienced blended classroom teachers because of the incorporation of reflective course design activities and principles.

A Step-by-Step Guide
The Blended Course Design Workbook can be used by an individual, in a group, or in consultation with an educational development or instructional technology professional. This book is written as a step-by-step guide to building your course and is meant to be read sequentially, with each new chapter building on the previous

chapters. Additionally, within each chapter are small activities that build on one another using a backward design structure (Wiggins & McTighe, 2005; see also, Chapter 1). In each chapter you will also find both pedagogical theory as well as concrete tasks to complete in order to design your blended course within one semester.

Your LMS Sandbox

It is recommended that you contact your academic computing department to see if you can have a "sandbox" space in your LMS. A sandbox is a practice space in your LMS that is separated from the live courses you may be currently teaching. This sandbox serves multiple purposes:

1. You can apply what you are learning in this book directly to an online classroom space, but without the pressure of practicing in front of a live audience.
2. You can practice a range of technologies that you might use in your blended course so that you feel comfortable with all the course tools before you introduce them to your students.
3. You can build your course step-by-step, using the guides at the beginning of each chapter to try out new tools, technologies, and organizational components within your LMS.

If you cannot get a "sandbox" LMS space to work within, consider signing up for a free LMS space where you can familiarize yourself with the tools available for blended learning. (For more information on free LMS spaces, see Chapter 7.)

Chapter Structure

The chapters in *The Blended Course Design Workbook* all have the following organizational structure:

What Do We Know About . . . ?: A short introduction of pedagogical theory and research literature relevant to the chapter's topic that helps contextualize the chapter within the larger course design process.

A Step-by-Step Guide to . . . : A series of guiding questions, worksheets, templates, and additional information to help you achieve the tasks recommended in each chapter.

Key Ideas: A summary of the key ideas is listed at the end of each chapter.

Questions for Faculty: A list of questions for faculty to ask to learn more about the chapter's topic at their institution is included at the end of each chapter.

Questions for Administrators: A list of questions for administrators to ask to learn more about the chapter's topic at their institution is included at the end of each chapter.

Documenting Your Course Design Progress: A graphic broken down by course design steps and additions that can be made within an LMS sandbox course if the reader has one available (Table I.3). Each chapter will end with a checklist of the course design components to be completed for each chapter. A full list of the tasks is included in Appendix D. Each chapter is designed to be completed within one week.

TABLE I.3.
Documenting Your Course Design Progress

Course Design Steps	In Your LMS Sandbox

A Note on the Authors
Some chapters in this book were single-authored and others coauthored, thus there will be references to both "I" and "we" throughout the text, depending on which chapter you are reading.

Additional Resources
Each chapter includes a variety of web resources as well as examples related to the chapter's topic. At the end of the book, additional examples and resources are included. Appendices include sample blended course syllabi, the full weekly course design task list, and a sample timed test support document. A glossary of terms as well as the full list of references for all chapters can be found at the end of the book. Digital copies of templates and worksheets can be accessed online (www.bcdworkbook.com).

Designing an effective blended course takes time, intentionality, and a clear sense of purpose. As you work through the activities and templates in the following chapters, remember to keep student learning at the center of your efforts. This workbook will help you to design your course, step-by-step, in manageable pieces. Each chapter has activities that encourage reflection along the way. Even though creating a new course (or redesigning an old one) can take a lot of work, I hope that you will enjoy the process and have some fun exploring the resources, technologies, and tools that can help make your blended course engaging, motivating, and innovative.

NOTES

I

FUNDAMENTALS OF BLENDED TEACHING AND LEARNING

What Do We Know About the Fundamentals of Blended Teaching and Learning?

Blended learning environments are similar in many ways to traditional classroom environments because a portion of the course is still held in a face-to-face setting. Thus, the course design process for blended environments will include many of the components found in the design of traditional courses: articulating course goals and learning objectives (this is covered in more detail in Chapter 2), creating clear expectations for students learning through assessments (see Chapters 3 and 4), designing effective learning activities (see Chapter 5), mapping your intended outcomes to align with assessments and learning activities (see Chapter 6), and crafting an effective syllabus (see Chapter 12). If you have previously designed a learner-centered course that is based on student learning objectives that are aligned with assignments and learning activities, there will be many similarities between your previous experience and the course design principles in this book. Even as formats for communicating with students and sharing information and learning activities may shift to accommodate new technologies within an online environment, an overall focus on helping students learn will remain at the center of your blended course design.

However, while blended learning environments share some similarities with traditional classrooms in terms of design, there are also components of blended environments that set them apart. Often, blended courses need additional attention to alignment in the design stage to ensure that the face-to-face and online activities are mutually supporting one another. Shea (2007) notes that "promoting, facilitating, and integrating online and face-to-face interactions are essential to blended learning. Without integration of interactions in the different modalities blended environments will fail to achieve their potential" (p. 26). This attention to alignment means that instructors may find that it is more important to prepare an entire blended course before the term begins rather than creating course components in the midst of the term, as can happen with more traditional course designs. Moreover, because of additional time online within the course structure, instructors need to prepare students for learning more autonomously and independently (this will be covered in more detail in Chapter 13). Adding technologies into the course can also change how students communicate with both the instructor and their peers. If students are engaging in blended learning for the first time, there may be some initial confusion about the format and course expectations. Considering these challenges from the outset can help to mitigate them before the course begins.

In the following sections, I elaborate on the importance of designing a course using backward design principles and explore how the blended environment brings about changing roles for teachers and students, including a shift from pedagogical to andragogical frameworks.

Backward Course Design for the Blended Classroom

Backward design (Wiggins & McTighe, 2005) is an approach to compiling a course that starts with the intended outcomes for student learning (see Figure 1.1). Instructors begin by reflecting on what students should know and be able to do upon successful completion of the course.

Then, based on these outcomes, instructors design assessments so that students can provide evidence of their learning. Learning activities and assignments are then created to help support each student's progress in the course and evaluate their level of learning (see Chapters 3 and 4 for more on assessing student learning in the blended environment).

Many instructors engage in some level of backward design instinctually, even if they have never heard of the philosophy before, because they are attempting to create a learning-centered course. An important component of backward design, however, is the setting aside of content until the intended outcomes are established. Not focusing on content coverage as a primary component of course design can be challenging for those who are new to backward design, but drafting intended outcomes first can help to ensure that your course planning keeps student learning at the center as you create and align different course elements. Each chapter of this workbook will help you to create a different piece of your course, aligning each component along the way.

Changing Roles of Teachers and Students: Pedagogy Versus Andragogy

Despite some fundamental similarities between traditional and blended environments, both instructors and students will notice significant changes in their roles in the classroom

Figure 1.1. The process of backward design.

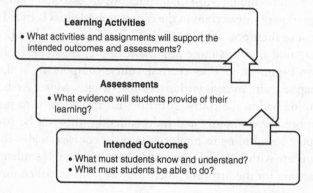

BOX 1.1
Best Practice Tip

When transitioning a traditional course to a blended model, instructors should be attentive to the credit hours for the course so they can ensure that students are not being asked to do extra online work for the same amount of credits. Rather than just adding online components to already existing course requirements, remember that online components in blended learning environments are intended to *replace* face-to-face time.

and in the online environment. One key shift is from a pedagogical environment to one that is more andragogical. Although many instructors use the term *pedagogy* as a catchall for describing their teaching strategies, *andragogy*, or teaching methods for adult learners (Knowles, 1980), might be a more appropriate description, particularly in the blended classroom. Even if you have never heard of andragogy before, if you have practiced student-centered teaching then you are probably using some of the methods and strategies of andragogy to engage and motivate your students. Based on Knowles' (1980) principles of andragogy, Caulfield (2011) articulated the differences between pedagogical and andragogical methods of teaching and learning for the blended classroom (see Table 1.1).

Andragogy becomes a central component of the blended environment because of the shift to online tools and technologies where students are being asked to do more learning on their own. Students in blended courses often must hone their time management skills, learn how to be more self-directed with the range of resources available to them online, and be more proactive about asking questions when they are confused with course materials. If online and face-to-face activities for the course are truly aligned, then prepared students will have a solid comprehension of the online content and will be able to actively participate in the in-class activities and discussions, and vice versa. Missing either component can disrupt the student learning experience and cause students to fall behind. Unfortunately, because of the fast pace of many blended courses, students who fall behind often find it difficult to catch up. (See Box 1.1 for a best practice tip related to student workload.)

As mentioned previously, instructors transitioning courses to a blended modality must be prepared to do much of the design work up front. It can also be challenging for some instructors to be more "hands-off" in the blended classroom because of the increase in autonomous student learning. Instructors may find themselves replacing more direct instruction, in which the teacher is primarily responsible for students' learning, with a guided inquiry model through which students take on additional responsibility for their learning. In the blended environment, instructors should also plan for additional time during the semester to communicate with students through the online tools in the course as well as via email. As Carroll-Barefield, Smith, Prince, and Campbell (2005) note, "often, online instructors are inundated with emails from students asking questions about assignments and tests when the answers to their questions are offered very prominently within the online course materials."

TABLE 1.1.
Principles of Pedagogy and Andragogy

Pedagogical Principles	*Andragogical Principles*
Learners learn what the teacher tells them they need to know	Learners need to know why information is important to learn; educators need to make this evident
Learning is the primary responsibility of the teacher	Learning is the primary responsibility of the learner
Transferring information is the most frequently used method of teaching, and learner experience is minimized	Drawing on the individual's personal experience and relating that experience to information from the discipline is the most frequently used method of teaching
Readiness to learn course content is determined by the teacher and uniformly applies to the entire class	Applying scaffolding techniques, such as group interaction, simulation, and case analysis, is frequently used to enhance each individual's readiness to learn
Content to be learned is determined by the logic of the discipline	Information is best learned when applied to real-life situations that are relevant to the learner
External motivators (grades, monetary rewards) are considered primary motivators of learning	Intrinsic motivators (self-esteem, need to achieve) are more important than extrinsic motivators

Caulfield, 2011, p. 9; © 2011, Stylus Publishing. Reproduced with permission.

A well-designed online environment can certainly impact this phenomenon, but less face-to-face time with students can result in an increase in online communication for instructors throughout the term, especially when students are new to the blended environment.

One area where instructors can intentionally articulate the balance between andragogy and pedagogy in their blended course is in how (and how much) they choose to incorporate the use of technology. As Christensen (2003) notes, "finding the right blend of online and face-to-face instruction is a balancing act for both instructors and students" (p. 242); this blend can take several iterations of a course to perfect. Creating or linking to tutorials for how to use foundational technologies for the course is one method to ensure student success. It is also recommended to not include too many technological tools in one course (particularly if those tools are new to the instructor) and instead focus on integrating one to three tools that are central to the course learning objectives. For example, an instructor may choose to augment in-class discussions by incorporating the online discussion board feature of an LMS, use video lectures to help communicate course content, and have students interact in small groups outside of class through the LMS chat feature.

As one scholar notes, the increase in student autonomy in the blended and online classroom means that "students also need to learn to study effectively online"

(Appana, 2008, p. 18). In addition to a student orientation to the blended learning structure and the main technologies to be utilized in the course, I also recommend that the instructor discuss how students can best succeed in the course through time management, self-directed learning, and taking advantage of in-class time to ask questions and clarify out-of-class work. Students should be informed of the differences of the blended method as soon as possible upon registering for a blended course. Several institutions have marked blended courses during the registration process and included a definition of *blended learning* in the course description so that students are well aware of what they are signing up for. Having the LMS site set up for students to access early is also a helpful way to introduce students to the course structure before they meet with an instructor face-to-face. Chapter 13 offers additional strategies to encourage student success in the blended classroom.

In the step-by-step guide that follows, you will have an opportunity to learn from blended instructors who have gone before you and explore your own plans for using pedagogical and andragogical principles and activities in the blended course you are designing. As you complete the activities in this chapter, use Table 1.2 to make notes on the similarities and differences you notice between traditional and blended courses.

TABLE 1.2.
Similarities and Differences Between Traditional and Blended Courses

Similarities	Differences

A Step-by-Step Guide to Fundamentals of Blended Teaching and Learning

As you embark on your blended course design work, take some time to reflect on the similarities and differences between your experiences designing and teaching traditional courses and the design steps for creating your new blended learning environments (use Table 1.2 as a template). This reflection will help you to decide what components are important to keep as well as what kinds of changes you may want to make as you transition your course to a blended modality.

Interviewing an Experienced Blended Course Instructor

Before you start designing your blended course, I recommend finding someone who has previously taught in the blended format (preferably on your campus, but another campus is also fine), so that you can learn from their experience. Here are some potential questions to get you started:

1. What changes have you noticed in the role of the teacher in the blended environment?

2. What changes have you noticed in the role of the student in a blended environment?

3. What has most surprised you about your experience teaching a blended course?

4. What kind of support was most helpful when you designed and implemented your blended course? What specific campus resources, units, offices, or people helped you?

5. What else would you like to share about your blended teaching experience (i.e., things you wish you had known, suggestions, encouragement, etc.)?

Exploring Pedagogical and Andragogical Principles

Based on the discussion of andragogy and pedagogy earlier in the chapter, where do you see components of within both your traditional courses and the blended course you are designing? There is a range of models for how you can incorporate both methods into your teaching in the blended classroom. For example, depending on the level of experience your students have with online learning, you may want to include intentional pedagogically oriented activities in the beginning until they feel comfortable with the technology and environment (see Figure 1.2). The level of your students (first-year students, seniors, graduate students) will also impact these choices.

Using Caulfield's (2011) descriptions of pedagogy and andragogy, Table 1.3 allows you to explore how you see particular pedagogical and andragogical principles occurring within the blended course that you are designing. (While you may not be able to entirely fill in Table 1.3 at this early stage of your course design, I encourage you to reflect on which components of your course are pedagogical and andragogical as you complete the remaining activities in the workbook. You may want to earmark this page and come back to it later.)

Figure 1.2. A spectrum of pedagogical and andragogical activities.

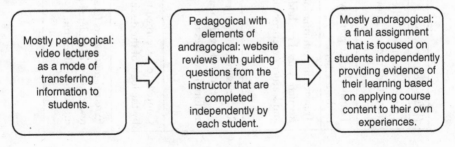

TABLE 1.3.

Applying Pedagogical and Andragogical Principles to Your Course

Pedagogical Principles	My Class	Andragogical Principles	My Class
Learners learn what the teacher tells them they need to know		Learners need to know why information is important to learn; educators need to make this evident	
Learning is the primary responsibility of the teacher		Learning is the primary responsibility of the learner	
Transferring information is the most frequently used method of teaching, and learner experience is minimized		Drawing on the individual's personal experience and relating that experience to information from the discipline is the most frequently used method of teaching	
Readiness to learn course content is determined by the teacher and uniformly applies to the entire class		Applying scaffolding techniques, such as group interaction, simulation, and case analysis, is frequently used to enhance each individual's readiness to learn	
Content to be learned is determined by the logic of the discipline		Information is best learned when applied to real-life situations that are relevant to the learner	
External motivators (grades, monetary rewards) are considered primary motivators of learning		Intrinsic motivators (self-esteem, need to achieve) are more important than extrinsic motivators	

As you begin the process of designing your course, it is important to keep in mind the fundamentals of blended teaching and learning discussed in this chapter. Employing the backward design process and reflecting on principles of pedagogy and andragogy will help you to build a sturdy foundation as you continue to layer in course design components through the activities included in the following chapters.

Key Ideas From Chapter 1

- Blended models of teaching and learning have important differences from traditional models.
- Backward design is a set of principles that can ensure that the creation of your blended course is student-centered.
- Knowing the differences between pedagogical and andragogical methods can help you to design appropriate learning activities that will best fit your students in a blended course environment.

Questions for Faculty

- What will be the biggest change for you in transitioning from a traditional to a blended course modality? What opportunities or challenges arise from this change?
- To what degree are the courses you teach pedagogical or andragogical? Do you think that your choices to be pedagogical or andragogical are discipline-specific?
- What level of experience do you have with backward course design? Will it be challenging to focus on design before content coverage? Why or why not?

Questions for Administrators

- How are students made aware that they are registered for a blended course?
- How are faculty assigned to teach blended courses on your campus?
- What resources do you have on campus (e.g., a teaching and learning center or an instructional technology group) that you can leverage to assist faculty with blended course design?
- What resources do you have on campus (e.g., a teaching and learning center or an instructional technology group) that you can leverage to assist faculty with learning the technologies they will need to use to successfully teach a blended course?

Documenting Your Course Design Progress

TABLE 1.4.
Documenting Your Course Design Progress

Course Design Steps	In Your LMS Sandbox
• Based on what you have read in this chapter, use Table 1.2 to reflect on the similarities and differences between traditional courses you have taught and what you envision for your blended course. • Complete an interview with an experienced blended course instructor to see what advice they can offer as you begin the blended course design process. • Explore the pedagogical and andragogical principles in your own teaching using Table 1.3. • If you will be redesigning a previously taught course, gather all of your course materials in one place (physically or digitally) for easy reference.	• Establish an LMS sandbox space to work in through your institution's academic computing or instructional design office.

NOTES

WRITING COURSE GOALS AND LEARNING OBJECTIVES

With Danny Fontaine

What Do We Know About Writing Course Goals and Learning Objectives?

Writing course goals and learning objectives is a foundational step in backward design that helps instructors establish the intended outcomes of their students' learning (Wiggins & McTighe, 2005). As introduced in Chapter 1, backward design is an approach to compiling a course that starts with the desired results, your goals, and what you want your students to learn or to become. Providing course goals and learning objectives gives students the organizational structure of your course and can help to hold instructors accountable to what they want to prioritize for student learning. Both goals and objectives should be student-centered rather than course-centered. Additionally, both course goals and learning objectives should reflect successful student performance.

The process of backward design is a helpful way to ensure that your intended outcomes, assessments (see Chapters 3 and 4 for more about assessing student learning), and learning activities are intentionally aligned (see Chapter 5).

The following are detailed descriptions of course goals and learning objectives that pay particular attention to the relationship among them.

Course Goals

1. Course goals reflect the larger ideas of what you want your students *to know and understand* through your course and are most successful when they are aligned with larger program goals, disciplinary goals, or professional standards.
2. Course goals are frequently not measurable and use verbs like "know" or "understand"; because they represent big ideas, they can be broad and vague.
3. Course goals reflect essential questions for your course and/or discipline.

Learning Objectives

1. Each learning objective should be connected to or stem from a course goal; in other words, course goals and learning objectives should be intentionally aligned.
2. Each learning objective should reflect what you want your students *to be able to do.*
3. Each learning objective should be measureable.

4. Each learning objective should be observable.
5. Each learning objective should target one specific aspect of student performance.

BOX 2.1
Best Practice Tip

Do: Upon successful completion of this course, students will know/understand/be able to . . .

Don't: This course will offer students . . . This course will provide students with . . .

BOX 2.2
Course Goal Examples

Upon successful completion of this course, students will *understand* the scientific method.

Upon successful completion of this course, students will *know* the components that comprise a successful marketing campaign.

BOX 2.3
Learning Objective Examples

Upon successful completion of this course, students will be able to *evaluate* sources of information.

Upon successful completion of this course, students will be able to *take a position* on a debatable historical issue.

Every course goal should have multiple learning objectives assigned to it. Course goals are measured through the assessments tied to learning objectives. Writing course goals is one way of connecting specific, measurable learning objectives back to the larger curriculum of your department. By assessing whether a student can complete or demonstrate different tasks and skills, you can evaluate their overall knowledge and understanding of the course material and the broader aims of your program or major. (See Boxes 2.1, 2.2, 2.3, and 2.4 for a best practice tip and examples of course goals and learning objectives.)

Intended outcomes, assessments, and learning activities work together to help you measure student learning (see Figure 2.1).

Some extra tips:

1. Try not to list multiple verbs in one objective—since each skill will be measured and assessed in a different way, each verb should be a separate objective.
   WRONG: Upon successful completion of this course, students will be able to *read* and *write* with a critical perspective.

BOX 2.4

Example of Course Goal and Accompanying Learning Objectives

Goal: Upon successful completion of this course, students will *know* the scientific method.

Objective 1: Upon successful completion of this course, students will be able to *list* the components of the scientific method.

Objective 2: Upon successful completion of this course, students will be able to *apply* the scientific method to a real-world question or problem.

Objective 3: Upon successful completion of this course, students will be able to *describe* their use of the scientific method to a nonscientist.

Figure 2.1. Components of measuring student learning.

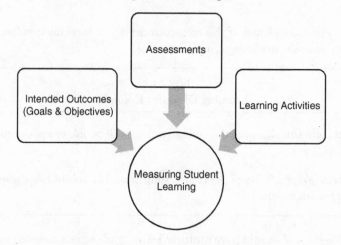

RIGHT: Upon successful completion of this course, students will be able to *read* from a critical perspective.

2. Do not use your assignments for your objectives. An assignment provides the evidence of a student's success with the objectives. Ideally, objectives should be measurable by more than one method, so if your objective can only be measured in one way, it is probably an assignment.
WRONG: Upon successful completion of this course, students will be able to *write a 20-page paper*.
RIGHT: Upon successful completion of this course, students will be able to *construct a thesis statement* with a clear and persuasive claim.

In the step-by-step guide that follows, you will have the opportunity to draft some essential questions for your course, as well as your course goals and learning objectives. The activities in the remainder of the chapter encourage reflection and iteration. You may need to complete multiple drafts before you feel satisfied with the goals and objectives that you articulate for your blended course.

A Step-by-Step Guide to Writing Course Goals and Learning Objectives

Step 1: Alignment With Department and Program Goals

As you begin the process of drafting goals and objectives, especially for a new course, your department-level program goals can be an excellent starting point. Program goals are typically those understandings and skills that your department has agreed students should graduate with after completing your program. Consider meeting with your department chair to discuss how the blended course you are designing fits into the larger curriculum to ensure alignment with larger goals. It can also be helpful to look at the prerequisites for the course you are designing as well as the courses that follow yours, and for which your course may serve as a prerequisite. If you are teaching a course that is part of a sequence, meeting with the colleagues who teach the other courses connected to yours can also help to shape and hone the goals and objectives you are drafting.

Step 2: Essential Questions

Wiggins and McTighe (2005) recommend locating the essential questions of a course as part of backward design; these questions "explicitly focus on the big ideas that connect and bring meaning to all the discrete facts and skills" (p. 105). Box 2.5 offers some examples of essential questions.

Essential questions for my blended course:

- _____
  _____
  _____

- _____
  _____
  _____
  _____

- _____
  _____
  _____

- _____
  _____
  _____

BOX 2.5
Essential Question Examples

How does constitutional law impact the day-to-day life of U.S. citizens?

What impact can one person have through the implementation of sustainable consumerism?

What is the relationship between culture and education?

Does global warming exist?

How does space influence the making of place?

Step 3: Questions for Writing Course Goals

Consider the following questions and choose two or three to respond to in the space provided on the following page. These questions should help bring the larger themes of your course and discipline closer to the surface as you prepare to draft your course goals.

1. Imagine what a group of graduating students (i.e., beginner, master level) who have taken your course would say. If they thought it was among the most valuable courses they have ever taken, what would they be saying about the course?
2. What do you want to provide for your students, what should they know/do/care about?
3. How is technology used by professionals trained in your discipline?
4. What is the appropriate level for your students to be able to function in the skill-sets offered by your course?
5. Do you need to take into account any general education curriculum goals that pertain to this course?
6. Do you need to take into account any licensure or accreditation goals that pertain to this course?
7. What areas of content should students be able to easily remember upon finishing this course?
8. What technology-related tools or skills should students be able to easily remember upon finishing this course?
9. What do you want students to get out of this blended course experience in addition to learning course content?

Pick two or three of the most relevant questions for writing course goals and respond to them in the space provided:

BOX 2.6
Example Learning Objectives for a Blended Course

Upon successfully completing this course, students will be able to do the following:

- Communicate effectively via email or discussion board
- Demonstrate an ability to persuade in an online environment
- Work with others in virtual settings
- Demonstrate proficiency with particular technologies important to a discipline or career
- Read about and understand research using online tools (e.g., surveys)
- Conduct research using online tools (e.g., surveys)
- Analyze online documents and/or situations (e.g., medical diagnoses, historical analyses)
- Negotiate in virtual settings
- Demonstrate competency with team-building skills such as cooperation, communication, and building trust in an online environment
- Access online information efficiently
- Evaluate sources (both primary and secondary) in an online environment

---

Step 4: Drafting Technology-Specific Learning Objectives

Consider the components of your course, any technologies you already plan to use, and the different ways that you would like students to communicate with one another in the course. Are there specific skills or attitudes that you want students to have in relation to technology? Look over the examples provided in Box 2.6 and write down any technology-specific learning objectives you plan to use in your course in the space provided. While technology-specific objectives are not a mandatory component of blended classrooms, they can be helpful if there are technology-specific skills that students will be expected to learn in order to be successful.

Technology-specific learning objectives for my blended course:

- _____
  _____

- _____
  _____

Step 5: Drafting Course Goals and Learning Objectives

Using Table 2.1, begin to write down your course goals and learning objectives for your blended course. (See Box 2.7 for a recommendation related to Table 2.1.) Do not feel like you have to fill all the open slots for potential course goals; usually three to five goals are sufficient for a three- to four-credit course (especially given

BOX 2.7
Course Design Recommendation

Photocopy Table 2.1 or download the digital template from www.bcdworkbook.com so that you can create multiple drafts of your course goals and learning objectives.

that each goal needs to be connected to multiple learning objectives). You will want to consider the appropriate number of learning objectives for your course given the level of your student population and what you think can reasonably be accomplished in the time that you have with those students. In my experience, instructors tend to overfill courses with learning objectives and content, so consider whether everything you plan to include is absolutely necessary. Remember that just because something is covered in a course does not mean that a student has learned it.

Also, keep in mind that drafting course goals and learning objectives can take time. Course goals and learning objectives can go through several iterations as you complete the rest of your course design, so do not feel like you need to have perfect goals and objectives before you continue on with your course design process.

To help you in the drafting process, please also refer to Box 2.8, which provides a sample list of verbs for writing learning objectives. This list of verbs is organized according to Bloom's Taxonomy, which offers a structured way of understanding the stages of cognition. The verbs associated with lower-order thinking skills are the easiest tasks, and the verbs associated with higher-order thinking skills are more difficult. If you would like to see additional examples of course goals and learning objectives, see the example syllabi included in Appendix C.

Your Course Goals and Learning Objectives

Use Table 2.1 to fill in the course goals and accompanying learning objectives for your blended course. Once you have a complete draft of your course goals and learning objectives, set them aside for a while and then revisit them with Table 2.2 as a guide for self-critique.

Chapter 12 will offer additional guidance for building your blended course syllabus and how you should include your goals and objectives. However, the syllabus is not the only place for goals and objectives to be communicated to students. As you complete the remaining chapters in the workbook consider the different places where you would like to communicate your course goals and learning objectives to your students throughout the course. In addition to the syllabus, you might also consider listing goals and objectives on assignments or including them in grading rubrics (see Chapter 3), creating a check-in conversation regarding goals and objectives for the course at mid-semester (consider including this in the course map you will build in Chapter 6), or collecting formative feedback from students regarding their self-assessment of their own progress regarding the course goals and objectives (see additional ideas for student self-assessment in Chapter 3 and Chapter 5).

BOX 2.8
What Is Bloom's Taxonomy?

The original draft of Bloom's Taxonomy was published in 1956 and was initially devised to help create a bank of test questions across a range of faculty who were trying to measure similar learning objectives. Educational psychologist Benjamin Bloom led this effort and, although the publication of *Taxonomy of Educational Objectives: The Classification of Educational Goals, Handbook I: Cognitive Domain* did not receive much attention at the time, Bloom's work is now one of the most widely used and cited taxonomies of student learning.

Bloom's Taxonomy is "a multi-tiered model of classifying thinking according to six cognitive levels of complexity" (Forehand, 2005). The taxonomy is meant to be applied in order, from lower levels of cognitive thinking in a step-by-step process toward higher levels of cognition. In the 1990s, a former student of Bloom, Lorin Anderson, revised the Taxonomy to include different terminology as well as a different order of the stages.

	Old Version (Bloom & Krathwohl, 1956)	**New Version** (with sample verbs) (Anderson & Krathwohl, 2001)
Higher Order Thinking Skills	Evaluation	Creating: producing, planning, designing
	Synthesis	Evaluating: critiquing, judging, testing
	Analysis	Analyzing: comparing, deconstructing, integrating
	Application	Applying: using, implementing, deploying
Lower Order Thinking Skills	Comprehension	Understanding: summarizing, explaining, classifying
	Knowledge	Remembering: listing, describing, identifying

Bloom's Taxonomy has also undergone revision as new technologies have changed student learning goals and objectives. Additional revisions of the Taxonomy have incorporated expanded definitions of *knowledge* and *cognitive process dimensions* to help illustrate how *what* is to be learned and *how* it will be learned are related (Heer, 2011).

When writing the learning objectives for your blended course, consider how an understanding of Bloom's Taxonomy can help you assess the level at which students need to learn in the course and the different processes (verbs) of learning that you want them to engage with in both online and face-to-face environments.

TABLE 2.1.
Your Course Goals and Learning Objectives

Course: _____	
Course Goal	*Learning Objective(s)*
1.	
2.	
3.	
4.	
5.	
6.	

(Continues)

TABLE 2.1. *(Continued)*

Course: _____	
Course Goal	*Learning Objective(s)*
7.	
8.	

TABLE 2.2.
Characteristics of Course Goals and Learning Objectives

	Course Goals	*Learning Objectives*
Measureable and observable		✓
Student-centered rather than course-centered	✓	✓
Reflects what you want your students to *be able to do*		✓
Connects to or stems from a course goal		✓
Reflects successful student performance	✓	✓
Uses broad language with verbs like *know* or *understand*	✓	
Reflects essential questions for your course and/or discipline	✓	
Targets one specific aspect of student performance ·		✓
Uses an appropriate action verb that targets the desired level of performance		✓

Key Ideas From Chapter 2

- Course goals and learning objectives represent the intended outcomes of your course.
- Course goals and learning objectives are foundational to an aligned course.
- Course goals and learning objectives are dependent on one another to ensure assessment of student learning.

- Learning objectives can reflect specific technologically-oriented skills in a blended course.
- Creating course goals and learning objectives is an iterative process that can take multiple drafts.

Questions for Faculty

- How are the goals and objectives that you drafted using this chapter different from or similar to those that you have used previously in your courses?
- Can you connect your course goals and learning objectives to your department's program goals or curricular objectives?
- How will you communicate your course goals and learning objectives to your students throughout the course (i.e., on the syllabus, listed on assignments, included in grading rubrics, a check-in conversation at mid-semester, formative feedback from students, etc.)?

Questions for Administrators

- Do you require faculty to provide course goals and learning objectives on a syllabus or other course document for students to access at the beginning of the term?
- What support does your institution have in place to help faculty write and revise their course goals and learning objectives each term (faculty development office, teaching and learning center, online resources, syllabus template, model examples, etc.)?

Documenting Your Course Design Progress

TABLE 2.3.
Documenting Your Course Design Progress

Course Design Steps	In Your LMS Sandbox
• Find a copy of your department's program goals and/or discuss the alignment of the program goals and your course with your department chair. • Brainstorm the essential questions for your course. • Decide whether your course will have technology-specific learning objectives. • Complete an initial draft of your course goals and learning objectives.	• Think about how and where you plan to communicate your course goals and learning objectives to students in your LMS sandbox.

NOTES

ASSESSING STUDENT LEARNING IN YOUR BLENDED COURSE

What Do We Know About Assessing Student Learning in Your Blended Course?

According to Suskie (2009),

> Assessment is the ongoing process of
> - establishing clear, measurable expected outcomes of student learning;
> - ensuring that students have sufficient opportunities to achieve those outcomes;
> - systematically gathering, analyzing, and interpreting evidence to determine how well students' learning matches the course expectations; and
> - using the resulting information to understand and improve student learning. (p. 4)

Maki (2010) similarly describes an assessment cycle that includes identifying outcomes, gathering evidence, interpreting that evidence, and implementing changes based on the interpretations.

Planning assessments for your blended course will not be all that different from what you do in a traditional classroom. You will still want to create activities and assignments that are aligned with your course goals and learning objectives (see Chapter 2), space out your assignments to afford students time to process and synthesize information, and create opportunities for formative and summative methods of assessment. Formative assessment methods are often low-stakes, not always graded "check-in" points to help you gauge student learning in the moment and make changes to future classes based on students' level of comprehension. Formative assessments can also help students with metacognition, or the process of intentionally reflecting on their own learning. Summative assessment methods are often more high-stakes, graded, and formal assignments to evaluate students' comprehension of the course material. For large summative assessments, it can be helpful to scaffold the assignment, or break it down into smaller parts for students to complete in manageable and sequential pieces. When possible, building in the opportunity for students to practice with low-stakes activities or assignments before completing a high-stakes assessment is recommended. Some examples of formative and summative assessment examples are listed in Table 3.1 (see also, Angelo & Cross, 1993).

TABLE 3.1.
Formative and Summative Assessment Examples

Formative Assessment Examples	Summative Assessment Examples
• Minute papers (short reflections where students respond to one or two questions regarding the course content for that day) • Discussions • Graphic organizers (a way to express knowledge visually that can also be used to illustrate the relationship between ideas or concepts; a common example is a mind map or brainstorming map) • Practice tests or assignments • Rough drafts • Peer or self-assessments • Journals or reflective writing	• Midterm or final exam • Paper • Final project • Portfolio • Statewide or national tests • Placement exams • Performances

BOX 3.1
Holistic Rubric Example

An "A" discussion board post will be thoughtful, include references to the course readings, and respond to more than one other post from a peer. A "B" discussion board post will include at least one reference to course readings and respond to at least one other post from a peer. A "C" discussion board post will include a reference to course readings, but the reference may be incorrect or unclear and only tangentially responds to a post from a peer. A "D" discussion board post will lack references to course readings and will not respond to any posts from peers. Students will earn a failing grade for not posting to the discussion board at all.

Creating rubrics for each of your assignments can serve as a helpful guide for students in your course. Rubrics are made up of criteria that (a) provide students with an understanding of your expectations and (b) offer feedback to students regarding their performance in the course. Often, rubrics are tied directly to course goals and learning objectives. Holistic rubrics may be written in paragraph or bullet formats and will describe criteria in an overall fashion (see Box 3.1). Analytic rubrics are often in a table format and will break down criteria into smaller parts (see Box 3.2).

Sharing rubrics with your students before they turn in assignments can help to guide students' work as well as provide a roadmap for success. Rubrics can also help students to better understand their strengths versus the areas that they need to give more attention for the next assignment. Rubrics provided ahead of time can also be utilized for peer- and self-assessment purposes for rough drafts before a final draft is submitted. Lastly, rubrics can be a huge time-saver for instructors when grading because the specific criteria for assessment is already drafted. Additional rubric

BOX 3.2
Analytic Rubric Example

	Excellent (A)	*Good (B)*	*Acceptable (C)*	*Revision Needed (D)*
Inclusion of Course Readings	Author includes multiple references to course readings	Author includes at least one reference to course readings	Author includes a reference to course readings, but the reference may be incorrect or unclear	Author lacks any references to course readings
Responding to Peers	Author responds to more than one peer	Author responds to at least one other post from a peer	Author only tangentially responds to a post from a peer	Author does not respond to any peers

examples can be found in Walvoord and Anderson (2010, pp. 107–114) and in Stevens and Levi (2005). The Association of American Colleges and Universities has also created 16 different VALUE rubrics that can serve as models for instructors who are creating their own assessment tools (learn more at www.aacu.org/value/rubrics).

A Step-by-Step Guide to Assessing Student Learning in Your Blended Course

As you prepare the assignments and assessments for your blended course, start with these guiding questions:

Assessment Breakdown: Guiding Questions

1. How can students best provide me with evidence of their learning?

2. Given the intended outcomes for my course (drafted in Chapter 2), are there aspects of student learning that will benefit from an online assessment?

Major Assignments: What Should Be Face-to-Face Versus Online?

Table 3.2 presents a translation for some common traditional assessment techniques used in the college classroom as you shift to a blended format. Box 3.3 explains why many of the suggestions in Table 3.2 are not one-to-one correlations (although some are).

TABLE 3.2.
Transitioning Traditional Assignment Techniques to a Blended Format

Bloom's Taxonomy	Face-to-Face (Traditional)	Blended
Knowledge	Ask students to complete a multiple choice question check-in test at the start of class.	Ask students to complete an online multiple choice question check-in test before the start of next class.
	Ask students to write a one-minute paper that gets them to recall the major themes from the previous class session.	Ask students to complete an online crossword puzzle that reinforces the main concepts from the previous class.
	Ask students to work in pairs to outline the major talking points from today's class.	Ask students to find two resources that pertain to topic X and post these resources to the class LMS site.
Comprehension	Ask students to write a summary essay that explains their interpretation of the assigned reading.	Ask students to listen to a podcast on topic X and to provide their own written interpretation on the class discussion board of the main message(s).
	Ask students to describe in their own words the main message of author X's reading in no more than three minutes at the start of class.	Ask students to create their own online concept map that shows how the main themes from an in-class discussion relate to one another.
	Ask students to draw a diagram or take a photograph that captures the essence of what was discussed in the previous class.	Ask students to contribute keywords to a glossary posted on the class LMS site.
Application	Ask students to construct an argument for or against topic X using the theories discussed in class.	Ask students to participate in an online simulation of topic X.
	Ask students to construct the key steps of X method as it relates to gathering data to understanding topic Y.	Ask students to pose three questions to the class discussion board that shows their application of the central themes of context X to context Y. Have students respond to each other's questions.

(Continues)

TABLE 3.2. *(Continued)*

Bloom's Taxonomy	Face-to-Face (Traditional)	Blended
Application	Ask students to find a headline news article that illustrates a key concept discussed in class. Have students bring in the newspaper article to class and explain to the class how the article demonstrates the concept they have selected.	Ask students to find an online headline news article that illustrates a key concept discussed in class. Have students post the newspaper article on the class LMS discussion board and explain to the class how the article demonstrates the concept they have selected.
Analysis	Ask students to compare two sets of data.	Ask students to compare the blog posts of author X and author Y on topic A in a discussion board post of their own on the class LMS site.
	Ask students to explain to the class the visual representation of data shown in graph X.	Ask students to conduct their own analysis on a set of online data. Have students post the results to the class LMS site with an explanation of their findings.
	Ask students to provide a detailed comparison of the writing style of author X in readings A and B.	Ask students to find two online articles that show a contrasting writing style of an author. Have students post these articles to the class LMS site with some guiding questions for their peers' exploration of the readings.
Synthesis	Ask students to generate a thesis statement based on the assigned readings.	Ask students to post their thesis statement to the class discussion board. Have students critique at least two of their classmates' statements.
	Ask students to design an ideal species to live in location Y based a set of conditions (e.g., climate) known to exist in location Y.	Ask students to watch two short online videos on topic X. Based on their observations from these videos ask students to outline a thesis statement to extend the understanding of the topic according to a set of research parameters. Have students post their statements to the class discussion board and offer feedback to at least three of their classmates' statements.

(Continues)

TABLE 3.2. *(Continued)*

Bloom's Taxonomy	Face-to-Face (Traditional)	Blended
Synthesis	Ask students to write a poem/song/short story that communicates their understanding of the material discussed in the previous class.	Ask students to design a wiki for a topic they are interested in and that is connected to the course material.
Evaluation	Ask students to critique the theoretical statement(s) of author X.	Ask students to create their own podcast (either on their own or in groups) that distills the main message of the readings for next class.
	Provide students with a logic puzzle based on the facts presented in class; ask them to solve this puzzle in groups.	Divide the class into two teams—one for and one against—a particular viewpoint of a current contentious debate. Have students debate with each other in their groups online to convince the opposing team why their viewpoint is the correct one.
	Ask students to write an editorial piece for a newspaper of their choice that presents their thoughts/reflections on topic X.	Ask students to complete an online (real-time updated) survey about topic X. Have students assess their own responses in comparison to the responses of the rest of the class.

BOX 3.3
Best Practice Tip

It is not always recommended to transition face-to-face activities to an online environment, even when a one-to-one correlation is available in an online format. For example, some instructors who wish to maintain a lecture format in their blended courses will choose to post a video of a one-hour lecture that was given in a face-to-face environment. Although this is technically a one-to-one correlation of the activity, the video may not be able to accomplish the same learning that would occur in a face-to-face environment where students can ask live questions. Just because a one-to-one correlation is available, that does not mean another, technology-enhanced option might not be better. In this situation, an instructor might want to re-record his or her lecture in smaller pieces, perhaps offering short online quizzes at the end of each one to help engage students in the material and to check their learning. (See Chapter 10 for more about creating multimedia components for your course.)

When shifting traditional classroom components to a blended format, think about your learning objectives (notice Table 3.2 is organized according to Bloom's Taxonomy; see Chapter 2) before deciding how best to incorporate the assessment into a blended classroom environment. You can use Table 3.3 (a blank version of Table 3.2) to think about what assignments might work well online versus face-to-face. The online tools described in Chapter 4 will also help you to decide what might work best as an online assessment.

You can start to map out the major assignments for your course using Table 3.4. Write down each learning objective for the course in the first column. Then, map out the formal assessments that will carry a percentage of the students' overall grades. As you map out these assignments, make a note about whether you think the assignment will take place in the traditional classroom or if it will be conducted as part of your students' work in the online component of your course. (If needed, you can read about online assessment tools in Chapter 4 before completing this step.) This map will allow you to see which learning objectives are not being formally assessed, as well as how many assessments will be occurring in-class versus online.

Now that you have the larger assignments mapped out for your course, you can decide where you can include smaller, low-stakes formative assessments using the template in Table 3.5. This template allows you to map out a schedule for the formative and summative assessments included in your blended course by week. In this map, you can decide whether they will be online or face-to-face and get a sense of the frequency of assessments across the term.

Guiding Questions and a Checklist for Overall Blended Course Assessment

Once you have mapped out your formal assessments and have created informal measures of student learning using the suggestions from earlier in this chapter, ask yourself the following questions about the overall plan that you have developed for assessing student learning:

1. Does this plan reflect how I can best assess my students' learning in this blended course?

2. Am I giving my students multiple opportunities to provide me with evidence that they are achieving the learning objectives of my blended course?

Table 3.6 offers a checklist for assessments in your blended course so that you can assess the overall plan that you have developed.

TABLE 3.3.
Template for Transitioning Traditional Assignments to a Blended Format

Bloom's Taxonomy	Face-to-Face (Traditional)	Blended
Knowledge		
Comprehension		
Application		
Analysis		
Synthesis		
Evaluation		

TABLE 3.4.
Assignment Mapping Template

Learning Objective to Be Assessed	Traditional Face-to-Face Assignment/ Assessment	Percentage/ Weight	Online Assignment/ Assessment	Percentage/ Weight

TABLE 3.5.
Template to Map Online and Face-to-Face Formative and Summative Assessments

Week	In-Class		Online	
	Formative	Summative	Formative	Summative
1				
2				
3				
4				
5				
6				
7				
8				
9				
10				
11				
12				
13				
14				
15				

TABLE 3.6.
Blended Course Assessment Checklist

	Yes	*No*	*Comments*
Is each one of my learning objectives measurable via some activity or assessment?	☐	☐	
Is each learning objective aligned with an activity/assignment/assessment that will assess my students' progress toward meeting this objective?	☐	☐	
Do I have a mix of individual and collaborative activities/assignments/assessments?	☐	☐	
Do I have a range of both online and traditional activities each week to develop my students' understanding of weekly course content?	☐	☐	
Do I have different kinds of online and traditional activities that develop my students' understanding of the course content?	☐	☐	
Do I have clear instructions for each activity explaining what I want students to do?	☐	☐	
Do I provide clear grading rubrics to guide my students' completion of the activity?	☐	☐	
Do I provide clear instructions for where students will find the online activities?	☐	☐	
Is there clear evidence of continual methods of assessment that are aligned with my learning objectives and that provide my students with informed feedback about their learning?	☐	☐	

Lastly, using Table 3.7, consider how each of your course goals are covered by the assessments you have planned for your students. This will help you to double-check that all of your course goals are being assessed and to look at assessment for the course as a whole. For each course goal, consider the ways you have planned to assess if and how the course is accomplishing this goal. These ways include the following:

- In-class activities
- Formal, graded assignments
- Exams or tests
- Online components
- Student feedback (i.e., self-assessments or formative assessments)

TABLE 3.7.
Mapping Course Goals and Assessments

Course Goal	In-Class Activities	Formal Assignments	Exams or Tests	Online Components	Formative Assessments

Key Ideas From Chapter 3

- Effective assessments of student learning are aligned with course goals and learning objectives.
- Instructors should plan a range of assessment activities that are both formative and summative.
- Mapping out assessment activities for the entire term can help instructors to ensure that they have a good balance between forms of assessment that will occur in class versus in an online environment.

Questions for Faculty

- What kinds of assessments do you already use in your traditional courses? Are these assessments something that could be transitioned for your blended course?
- Do you already use a mix of formative and summative assessments in your traditional courses? What ratio do you find works best to ensure student learning throughout the term?

Questions for Administrators

- Does your institution have a teaching and learning center, research office, or assessment group that could help faculty members develop assignments or assessment tools to measure student learning in a blended environment?
- As you get blended courses off the ground, what kinds of institutional-level data will need to be collected to measure student learning?
- Do you have an institutional research office or assessment committee that could aid in the collection of data from blended courses?
- What are the most important components of blended courses that you will want to measure?

Documenting Your Course Design Progress

TABLE 3.8.
Documenting Your Course Design Progress

Course Design Steps	In Your LMS Sandbox
• Using the reflection questions in this chapter, consider which assessments will best measure student learning in your blended course. • Using Table 3.3, decide which of your assignments will be fully online, fully in-class, or a mix of both online and in-class components. • Map the major assignments for your course using Table 3.4. • Complete Table 3.5 to map out your formative and summative assessments in a weekly schedule. • Apply the checklist in Table 3.6 to your course assessment plan. • Review the overall assessment plan and how it relates to your course goals using Table 3.7. • Create the assignments and assessments from Table 3.4 and Table 3.5. • Create rubrics, as appropriate, for your assignments using the tools and templates provided.	• Build an assignment in your LMS sandbox (there may be a special tool for this). • Find out if your LMS has a rubric tool and decide whether you plan to use it within your course. • Begin to explore the Grade Book function included in your LMS, and find out if there are training opportunities or online resources to learn how to use this tool.

NOTES

ONLINE ASSESSMENT TOOLS

With Linda Bruenjes

What Do We Know About Online Assessment Tools?

While research on online assessment is still in its beginning stages, various studies have explored the use of assessment tools in the online environment (see Quality Matters, 2015). However, as Cheng, Jordan, Schallert, and the D-Team (2013) argue, "assessment of online learning requires a thorough reconsideration given that the online learning environment is distinctly different from the traditional face-to-face classroom and brings new challenges to assessment" (p. 52). One of the benefits of a blended classroom is the instructor's choice of whether to offer assessments in the face-to-face classroom (which can mitigate concerns that instructors may have about students' cheating on exams taken outside of class) or in the online environment (which can free up face-to-face class time for other activities). As you plan the assessments for your blended course, you will want to consider whether and how you will integrate online assessment tools.

One subset of the research regarding online learning assessment is devoted to instructors' concerns regarding cheating, plagiarism, and the ethical behavior of students online (e.g., see Beck, 2014; Brothen & Peterson, 2012; Graham-Matheson & Starr, 2013; LoSchiavo & Shatz, 2011; Moten et al., 2013). There is a widespread perception that the online environment enables cheating, yet researchers have found that the incidence of cheating is no different than what is found in the face-to-face learning environment (Beck 2014; Varvel, 2005). Research does suggest, however, that increased use of "technology and the Internet can both facilitate cheating" (McNabb & Olmstead, 2009, p. 210), and that incidences of academic dishonesty, such as plagiarism, are harder to prevent in an age of digital learning. There are, however, plagiarism detection tools as well as alternative assessment strategies that you can choose to help mitigate cheating in the blended learning environment.

While many instructors have concerns about incidents of cheating increasing in online environments, Black, Greaser, and Dawson (2008) found that students have the opposite opinion, with "a vast majority of students (81%) feel[ing] that cheating within their online course is no more prevalent then cheating within a traditional course" (p. 28). In a study by Jones, Blankenship, and Hollier (2013), the majority of students surveyed reported never engaging in cheating-related activities such as "having another person take an online exam for you . . . , consulting with other people during an online exam . . . , [or] saving or copying an online exam for future use" (p. 265). However, students in this study did note that two specific areas, "using an open book during on online exam" and "using personal or class notes during an online exam" did not constitute cheating for them (p. 266). This study illustrates the importance of discussing and establishing what your expectations are for students who are taking an online exam regarding the resources they are permitted to use while engaging in the assessment activity.

Online Assessment Tools

There are several different kinds of online assessment tools that can help you to measure student learning, particularly within your LMS. The most time-saving features included in an LMS are the assessment tools, which offer the possibility of providing instructor feedback to students as they complete online assignments and automatic grade calculation for many different kinds of evaluation. In addition, there are an array of plagiarism detection tools that can also be used for peer review, student evaluation, and plagiarism education. The following are some of the most common tools available:

Surveys

Typically ungraded, surveys allow for anonymous collection of student responses and may be reused in a course or across courses. Some faculty use surveys within the LMS to collect formative feedback, such as "one minute" papers (Angelo & Cross, 1993) midterm student feedback, and group project preferences, throughout the course. Surveys can also be used to collect anonymous feedback regarding sensitive course topics.

Journals

Either graded or ungraded, depending on your learning objectives, journals can be used for student reflection, self-assessment, or other forms of assessment. Typically, the journal tool in an LMS allows for students' entries to be shared privately between just the student and the instructor.

Wikis and Blogs

Collaborative tools such as wikis and blogs can be used to assess group interactions as well as give the instructor a view as to how students are integrating their new knowledge with established concepts. You may also choose to use a free stand-alone blog or wiki (see Chapter 11 for more information on blogs and other forms of social media).

Tests and Quizzes

Typically graded, the test feature includes multiple question formats and feedback options so instructors can design formative or summative assessments to closely fit the course learning objectives. Your LMS may also include an option to generate unique ordering patterns for test items for each student to help mitigate concerns about students taking quizzes or tests in the same location and sharing answers. Tests and quizzes can also be used to help students self-assess and/or prepare for the next in-class meeting.

Assignment Submission

This feature allows instructors to track students' submissions of an assignment, offer private feedback, and track grades. Some LMSs offer special features such as automatically creating the assignment column in your grade book once an assignment is created or one-click downloading of all submitted assignments to your computer for easy access to students' work.

Rubrics

Some LMSs offer instructors the opportunity to build an electronic rubric that can be linked to specific assignments, shared with students, and used to evaluate student learning. (See Chapter 3 for additional information on creating rubrics.)

Plagiarism Detection

Depending on the LMS, you may have access to plagiarism reports such as "TurnItIn" or "SafeAssign" where students submit their work and have it checked for plagiarism as a part of the submission process. These reports are generated based on a database of assignments collected by the company that includes web-based writing, assignments being turned in by students at your institution, and assignments completed at other institutions using the plagiarism detection tool.

Grade Book

To help instructors calculate student grades, LMSs frequently include a digital grade book where student assessments can be recorded and collected. Grade books can be shared with students or remain private to the instructor. Assignments created using an LMS tool such as those described previously can often be linked directly to the grade book for ease of grading.

Analytics

Some instructors choose to set up a feature to monitor student engagement with course materials by tracking the frequency of student use of materials, length of student visits to the course LMS, and student progress with online assessments. Analytics features collect data to help instructors monitor student performance so that instructors can better understand how their students interact with course materials and activities. For example, an analytics report can show the most popular times that students are logging on to complete course work. They might also help an instructor understand why students are not prepared for in-class components because of information about whether students have been accessing the course site or materials posted there.

Additional online assessment tools outside of your LMS are designed to help you evaluate student learning and efficiently provide feedback to students. The following are some common tools that are available for these purposes:

Publisher Resources

Many publishers are creating online assessment tools to supplement textbooks. These online assessment tools may include quizzes, problem sets, or exam questions (see also, Chapter 9 and Box 4.1 for an important note on accessibility).

BOX 4.1
Accessibility Note

Although publisher resources can be an incredible addition to a blended course, it is important to check with your institution's disability services professionals to make sure that the online materials are accessible for all learners. For example, some adaptable learning technologies can be difficult for screen-readers to translate to learners who have visual impairments.

Rubistar

Rubistar is a website that helps instructors create rubrics for assignments, projects, and presentations. Although the site was originally designed for K–12 instructors, its features are also helpful to users in higher education. On the website, there are examples of rubrics for different kinds of projects such as debates, lab reports, and art projects. Users can start from a template provided in the website, or create a new rubric from scratch. Templates can also be modified to fit an instructor's specific assignment modifications.

Microsoft Word Track Changes

Microsoft Word offers the option of revising or responding to a piece of writing using "Track Changes," which highlights changes made by one user on another user's piece of writing. Changes are highlighted in a different color text to make edits or revisions clear to read. This feature also includes a "comment" option so that a user can add in comments to the side of the original text in order to make suggestions or ask questions. Many instructors use this feature to provide feedback on students' work when it is submitted in a digital format. Instructors can save the comments and send the document back to the student for review.

Concept Mapping

Concept Maps (also called "mind maps") are graphic organizers of knowledge that can be used to assess student learning. A number of free and low-cost concept mapping online tools such as bubbl.us, Cmap, vue.tufts.edu, and Inspiration.com are available. Concept maps allow students to synthesize and demonstrate their awareness of connections among a variety of concepts, theories, people, ideas, and other aspects of your course content.

Webquests

Webquests are organized individual or group scavenger hunts. Developed by Bernie Dodge at San Diego State University, these inquiry-based assignments typically offer embedded rubrics for assessing student learning (learn more at www.webquest.org).

If you would like your students to engage in peer assessment or collaborative assessment (Palloff & Pratt, 2009, pp. 36–39), consider integrating a tool such as Google Drive, where students can upload documents and offer comments and edits on each other's work. A tool like Google Drive also allows two students to look at and edit the same document simultaneously if you wanted to build in a real-time peer consultation on a project or paper into the online component of your course. LMS tools such as the discussion board can also help students engage in peer assessment more informally since students can see and respond to their peers' comments, ideas, and arguments asynchronously. If you choose to have your students assess each other's work, consider offering them a rubric tool with criteria for the assignment (see Chapter 3) to help guide the peer assessment process.

A Step-by-Step Guide to Online Assessment Tools

To help your students understand your expectations regarding academic dishonesty and cheating, it can be helpful to outline your own beliefs. As you answer the following questions, consider when in your course you might talk with your students about these issues and whether it will be done in writing (perhaps through the syllabus; see more in Chapter 12) or verbally in class.

Cheating and Academic Dishonesty: Guiding Questions

- For this course, can students respond to any of the assessments with an "open book" or "open note" approach?

- Do I have any underlying assumptions regarding how students will use the Internet during online assessments?

- Do I have any underlying assumptions regarding how and whether students will communicate with their peers during online assessments?

- Will I require the use of plagiarism software for written work in this course?

- Are there any assessments in this course that I feel strongly should be completed face-to-face to mitigate the possibility of cheating or academic dishonesty?

- Do I know the university policies regarding cheating and academic dishonesty in the online environment?

- Do I feel confident that I could determine whether students have cheated during an online assessment?

Gathering Student Feedback

At the beginning of your course, consider asking your students about their definitions of *cheating* and *academic dishonesty* so that you can correct any misalignments with your own beliefs and expectations for the course. This feedback could be gathered through a large-group conversation or an anonymous survey where you share the results with the class. Here are some example questions that could be included for either format:

- How do you define *cheating* when you are completing homework or assignments online?
- What are the best ways that an instructor can help you to know what cheating means in their course?
- What kinds of ways have you seen other students cheat in the online environment?
- Do you think that online cheating is a pervasive problem?

Preparing Students for Real-Time Assessments

If you plan to conduct real-time assessments online such as timed quizzes or exams, you will want to make sure that you do the following before, during, and after the assessment to help promote student success:

Before

Test out the assessment before releasing it to students.   Try out the assessment yourself to make sure the questions make sense, there is enough time to complete the assessment, and there are no technological issues that you need to troubleshoot. Your students will already be nervous about the quiz or exam, so you do not want them to have to worry about a technological issue if you can prevent it ahead of time.

Create a troubleshooting guide for students.   Whatever you do to develop a seamless experience for your students with online assessments, something will probably go wrong. A student's computer could freeze, the exam could time out unexpectedly, the wireless connection could be unstable, or students could receive some kind of error message when trying to submit answers. If you know about these things ahead of time (by testing out the assessment yourself first) you can advise students about how to respond to these issues by creating a troubleshooting guide. (An example guide is included in Appendix E.)

Prepare students in-class.   Talking with students in person about upcoming online assessments will help them know what to expect and allow them to ask questions. If possible, walk students through a sample quiz or exam in class so that they can see what the platform and structure will look like. This will also allow students to ask any questions they might have about the assessment or the online platform.

During

Be available via email during the real-time assessment.   Make sure to schedule the quiz or exam during a time that you are available via email in case students run into any problems, cannot access the assessment, or have other questions or concerns during the assessment.

After

Consider gathering feedback from students.   This will help you learn more about their experience of the process of completing the assessment. Student feedback can be especially helpful if it is the first time you are trying a new online assessment tool. Ask students if there was anything confusing about the process, whether they had enough time to complete the assessment, and if there is anything you can do in the future to make the process better for them.

Key Ideas From Chapter 4

- Instructors and students have different beliefs about what it means to cheat online; it is important to discuss and establish your expectations for students who are taking an online exam or other assessment to make sure there is no confusion.
- There are pros and cons to using online assessment tools.
- The blended environment offers instructors flexibility regarding when and where they would like to conduct assessments of student learning.

- Instructors should prepare students as much as possible when using online assessment tools so that technology troubleshooting issues do not impede students when they are providing evidence of their learning.

Questions for Faculty

- What is your prior experience using online assessment tools? Are online assessments something you feel comfortable integrating into your blended course?
- What concerns do you have, if any, about using online assessment tools? How might the blended environment, particularly the face-to-face time you will have with students, help to mitigate these concerns?

Questions for Administrators

- Does your institution have any policies about the use of online assessment tools, particularly regarding the use of these tools for summative exams?
- What kind of support structure does your institution provide for students regarding technology troubleshooting?

Documenting Your Course Design Progress

TABLE 4.1.
Documenting Your Course Design Progress

Course Design Steps	In Your LMS Sandbox
• Decide whether you plan to use online assessment tools within your course. • For any online assessment tools you choose to use, create a troubleshooting guide for students. • Think about how you will talk with students about your expectations for online assessments to ensure students will understand what constitutes cheating or academic dishonesty. • Consider whether and how you will collect feedback from students regarding their perceptions of what cheating means in an online environment. • Review the activities from Chapter 3 and add in any additional notes based on what you have learned from Chapter 4.	• If you plan to use specific online assessment tools, contact your academic computing office to explore how the tools can be integrated within your LMS. • In your sandbox, set up the online assessment tools so that you can test the tools to ensure they are working as you intend. • Post any troubleshooting guides that you create for students in your LMS sandbox. • If you decide to collect feedback from students using an online survey, create that survey in your LMS sandbox.

NOTES

5

DESIGNING EFFECTIVE
LEARNING ACTIVITIES

What Do We Know About Designing Effective Learning Activities?

One of the benefits of the blended course modality is the possibility for additional active learning in the face-to-face environment. *Active learning* has been defined in several ways, but a fundamental component of active learning is the argument that "students learn by doing" (Bowen, 2012, p. 192). Bonwell and Eison (1991) define *active learning* as "involving students in doing things and thinking about what they are doing" (para. 2). Others, such as Prince (2004), have defined *active learning* more specifically as "introducing student activity into the traditional lecture" (p. 3) and "promoting student engagement" (p. 4) more broadly. *Active learning* has also been defined as a "learner-centered" approach in which "the facilitator's job is to support everyone in doing his or her best thinking and practice" (Doyle, 2011, p. 53). Within the active learning paradigm, the role of the teacher as expert remains the same, but the approaches to help students learn will change to ensure that students are actively "doing" the learning in the course rather than passively receiving information. Through active learning, classroom activities transition from being teaching activities to being learning activities.

Analyses of the research on active learning have presented encouraging findings. Prince (2004) and Michael (2006) both ask a version of the following question: How do we know that active learning works? Prince (2004), who focuses on active learning components such as active lectures and collaborative, cooperative, and problem-based learning in the context of engineering education, reports that "although the results vary in strength, this study has found support for all forms of active learning examined" (p. 7). Michael (2006), who explores "evidence from the learning sciences, cognitive science, and educational psychology" (p. 160) in the context of teaching physiology, finds "there IS evidence that active learning, student-centered approaches to teaching physiology work, and they work better than passive approaches" (p. 165). Active learning approaches, perhaps because of their student-centered focus, are successfully helping students learn.

Within the research on active learning is a subset of literature that questions whether the traditional lecture can still be considered effective in light of what we know about active learning methods. Although critiques about lecture as a "passive" form of student engagement remain, the literature also points out the various advantages that lecture can provide such as "enabl[ing] the instructor to supplement the textbook by providing cutting-edge material" (Millis, 2012, p. 1) and providing "a place to question, identify, and undermine assumptions from the readings or that students bring to class" (Bowen, 2012, p. 189), among others. While lecture should not be the baby that is thrown out with the bathwater, the lecture method can be modified to take advantage of the benefits of active learning. This format is often called "active lecturing" in which instructors embed their lectures with questions for the class in the form of discussion or quizzes, short pair or group activities for students to apply what they are learning, modeling, or demonstration. Nilson (2010) offers additional concrete strategies for "making the lecture a learning experience" (p. 113) including giving students case studies to discuss, asking students to compare and contrast two elements from your lecture, and asking students to paraphrase elements from the lecture into their own words. For more information on transitioning lecture components online, see the information provided in Chapter 10 on creating multimedia resources.

An additional method of modifying the traditional lecture has been through the "flipped" model of teaching. In a flipped classroom, content delivery (e.g., a video lecture) is offered through the online components of the course so that more active learning can take place in the face-to-face classroom. The flipped model allows students to receive content as part of their homework and then engage with that content through various other online activities (e.g., a discussion board post, online quiz, or short writing assignment) before coming to class. While there is not an extensive literature base on the effectiveness of the flipped classroom (Abeysekera & Dawson, 2015; DeLozier & Rhodes, 2016), Abeysekera and Dawson (2015) have suggested that the flipped classroom approach can "be thought of as building upon sound theory and evidence from elsewhere" (p. 1). One of the areas of research that the flipped model of teaching draws from is the literature on active learning in the classroom.

There are three additional areas that can be especially helpful to consider when choosing learning activities for your blended course: direct instruction and guided inquiry, group activities, and metacognitive activities. In the remainder of this section, each of these areas is outlined in further detail.

Direct Instruction and Guided Inquiry

When instructors are designing a blended modality that includes active learning approaches, one thing to consider is the balance between direct instruction and guided inquiry. Direct instruction is often primarily instructor-led learning where students depend on the instructor for information or instructions to move forward. McTighe and Wiggins (2004) provide this question to help with the design of direct instruction: "What information or skills need to be taught explicitly to equip students to achieve the desired results for their expected performance?" (p. 218). Common forms for direct instruction can include face-to-face or video lecture, modeling, demonstration, or tutorials. (Box 5.1 offers an example of direct instruction.)

Guided inquiry is often primarily student-led learning where students will autonomously explore course materials with only minimal instructions or direction from the instructor. Guided inquiry can help students to engage in learning activities

BOX 5.1
Direct Instruction Example

An instructor finds that her students are consistently providing incorrect citations in their papers despite the fact that she has given them numerous online links to the citation style that is appropriate for the course. To help her students learn the correct citation style, the instructor creates an online video tutorial that demonstrates the different components of a correct citation and models the revision of an incorrect citation to one that is correct. Students are then asked to complete a citation style quiz to assess their understanding of the tutorial.

BOX 5.2
Guided Inquiry Example

For an end-of-course assignment, students are asked to complete a research paper on a topic of their choice. The instructor has designed the paper assignment so that students will complete the work in stages with small pieces of the assignment due at regular intervals. The instructor offers a basic framework for the assignment, and makes the deadlines for each piece clear, but expects that students will conduct the research for the paper and complete each stage of the project independently. The instructor has created a discussion board on the course website for students to post their questions about the project.

BOX 5.3
Learning Activities and Social Presence

In the blended environment, both direct instruction activities and guided inquiry should also be embedded with elements of social presence, or intentional activities and elements of the online environment that ask students to communicate and interact with the instructor or their peers. (You can read more about social presence in Chapter 8.)

such as experimentation, taking risks, creating, and collaboration. Common forms of guided inquiry might include face-to-face or online group work, independent research activities, or lab work. (Box 5.2 offers an example of guided inquiry.)

To be most effective, learning activities that include direct instruction or guided inquiry should contain active learning components that encourage students to engage in, and reflect on, what they are learning. (See Box 5.3 for connecting learning activities with social presence.)

Group Activities

Depending on the intended outcomes for your blended course (see Chapter 2), group activities can be a rich mode of learning activity for your students. There are

BOX 5.4
Four Kinds of Group Work Defined

Collaborative Learning	*Cooperative Learning*
Definition: "In collaborative learning, the focus is on working with each other (but not necessarily interdependently) toward the same goal. . . . Toward the discovering, understanding, or producing knowledge" (Davidson & Major, 2014, p. 21)	**Definition:** "Students work and learn together actively in small groups to accomplish a common goal in a mutually helpful manner" (Davidson & Major, 2014, p. 14); this group work can be structured or unstructured.
Examples: Reports or presentations in which tasks are split among group members	**Examples:** Jigsaw activities; Think/Pair/Share
Team-Based Learning (TBL)	*Problem-Based Learning (PBL)*
Definition: "TBL shifts the focus of instruction away from the teacher as dispenser of information and instead places the focus on students actively engaging in activities that require them to *use* the concepts to solve problems. . . . *Every* aspect of a TBL course is specifically designed to foster the development of self-managed learning teams" (Michaelsen, Davidson, & Major, 2014, p. 58).	**Definition:** "PBL fosters the ability to identify the information needed for a particular application, where and how to seek that information, how to organize that information in a meaningful conceptual framework, and how to communicate that information to others" (Duch, Groh, & Allen, 2001, p. 7). PBL is often interdisciplinary with "real world" applications.
Examples: Flipped classroom model	**Examples:** Case method; Simulated client interaction

several different kinds of group work that you can explore, but four common forms are collaborative, cooperative, team-based, and problem-based learning (see Box 5.4).

Importantly, these four modes of group work have distinctly different purposes (see Table 5.1).

If you decide to implement one of these group work approaches into your course, consider which method best aligns with your course learning objectives and the kinds of skills that you want your students to practice. Table 5.2 offers some examples of course goals and learning objectives for collaborative, cooperative, team-based, and problem-based learning, and Box 5.6 offers a best practice tip for setting up effective groups.

Group work is a flexible learning activity that can be completed face-to-face, online, or both (see Box 5.5 and also Chapter 7 for more information about online tools that might help you design group work activities online).

Group work can also help students to practice and hone a wide range of skills across a broad array of disciplines.

TABLE 5.1.
Defining Features Matrix for Four Kinds of Group Work

	Collaborative Learning	*Cooperative Learning*	*TBL*	*PBL*
Causal research supports a positive influence on student learning		✔	✔	✔
Used most extensively in the humanities and social sciences	✔			
Used most extensively in STEM fields		✔		
Used most extensively in health professions				✔
Can be designed at all levels of Bloom's Taxonomy	✔	✔	✔	✔
Focus is on interdependence		✔	✔	✔
Focus on individual accountability and responsibility		✔	✔	✔
Can use assigned group roles		✔	✔	✔
Overtly teaches group interaction, reflection, and/or processing skills		✔	✔	
Teams are mostly self-managed	✔		✔	

Note. Based on information from Davidson and Major (2014) and Michaelsen, Davidson, and Major (2014).

To learn more about collaborative, cooperative, team-based, or problem-based learning, I recommend the special issue on small group learning in the *Journal on Excellence in College Teaching* (Davidson, Major, & Michaelsen, 2014).

Metacognitive Activities

A foundational component of active learning is the inclusion of time and space for students to reflect on their learning. Metacognition, or the process through which students reflect on their own learning, can help students identify their strengths as well as areas where they may need additional practice or support. Stein and Graham (2014) note that metacognition can be especially impactful in blended courses "in

TABLE 5.2.
Course Goals and Learning Objectives for Four Kinds of Group Work

Collaborative Learning
Goal: Upon successful completion of this course, students will know/understand the characteristics of effective collaboration. **Objective:** Upon successful completion of this course, students will be able to consider the contributions of others.
Cooperative Learning
Goal: Upon successful completion of this course, students will understand the dynamics of effective group communication. **Objective:** Upon successful completion of this course, students will be able to contribute questions or concerns in a respectful way.
TBL
Goal: Upon successful completion of this course, students will know/understand the importance of a shared goal. **Objective:** Upon successful completion of this course, students will be able to develop a common goal.
PBL
Goal: Upon successful completion of this course, students will better understand the importance of approaching problems in a real-life context. **Objective:** Upon successful completion of this course, students will be able to apply the problem-based learning cycle (identify facts, generate hypothesis, identify knowledge deficiencies, apply new knowledge, abstraction, evaluation) to a unique situation (see Hmelo-Silver, 2004).

which past learning is made visible to students through their digital footprints in the online course environment" (p. 21). Fink (2003) also includes "learning how to learn" as one component needed to create a "significant learning experience" (p. 30). Unfortunately, the research shows that "students tend not to apply metacognitive skills as well or as often as they should" (Ambrose et al., 2010, p. 202). The following metacognitive learning activities can be included in a blended course in either face-to-face or online environments (see Chapter 7 for specific online tools that may help to integrate these activities into your online course environment).

Self-Assessment
Ask students to reflect on how well they think they did on a particular task or assignment. If you created a rubric for a particular assignment (see Chapter 3), you can ask students to fill out the rubric themselves to turn in along with their final product. If you do not have a rubric, ask students to respond to some reflective questions about

BOX 5.5
Online Tools to Assist With Group Work

The following tools can assist with organizing group work in an online environment. Some of these tools are free and others are fee-based but offer some kind of free trial. Always check with your campus academic computing office to see if your institution has licenses for these or similar products. Your LMS (read more in Chapter 7) may also have tools that can help organize group work.

- Basecamp (https://basecamp.com)
- CATME (http://info.catme.org)
- Dropbox (www.dropbox.com)
- Google Drive (www.google.com/drive)
- Google Teamwork (www.teamwork.com/googleapps)
- Trello (https://trello.com)
- Wiggio (https://wiggio.com)

The following tools can assist with online group communication:

- Google Hangouts (https://hangouts.google.com)
- Slack (https://slack.com)
- Skype (www.skype.com/en)
- TEAMMATES (https://teammatesv4.appspot.com/index.html)

BOX 5.6
Best Practice Tip

Setting up effective groups in a blended course involves many of the same components as when groups are used in the traditional classroom. For example, when creating student groups, be intentional. Barkley, Major, and Cross (2014) offer an excellent resource on methods for forming groups as well as specific learning activities that can best engage students in collaboration with one another.

their work, such as what was the most difficult part of the assignment for them and why? What parts of the assignment do they feel the most confident about and why?

Journaling

Student journals, whether private or shared with the instructor, can be a helpful way for students to process the learning experiences that they are having in your course. Stevens and Cooper (2009) offer an excellent resource on integrating the practice of journaling into the classroom. Journal assignments can be free form, or instructors can provide specific questions for students based on the course content.

Revision

Asking students to revisit their previous work for the purpose of revision can offer an opportunity for metacognitive learning activities. This kind of learning activity can be particularly impactful if students at the end of the course review work that they completed at the very beginning. When students revise work, ask them to first reflect on the kind of feedback they have received from the instructor or their peers before proceeding. You can also offer guiding questions such as what kinds of patterns do students notice in the feedback they have received or in the components of their work that requires revision?

Annotation

For readings assigned as homework or for the review of their peers' work, ask students to annotate as they complete the assignment. Students can be provided with specific things to note such as when they are confused, when they do not recognize a word, when they agree or disagree with what they are reading, or when what they are reading prompts a question for them. Instructors can also share their own annotations as a model for students.

Post-Exam Reflection

After a high-stakes exam or test, ask students to reflect on how they prepared. What kinds of study skills did they employ? What did they consider to be the study tasks that helped them the most? How much time did they spend studying for the exam or test? This kind of reflection, whether private or as a group, can help students to think about how the choices they make impact their learning.

A Step-by-Step Guide to Designing Effective Learning Activities

In the step-by-step guide that follows, you will have the opportunity to reflect on the kinds of direct instruction and guided inquiry activities you already use in your courses, which learning activities will be the best fit for your blended course given your intended outcomes and assessments, and how to decide which activities should be offered in the face-to-face versus online environment.

What Kinds of Activities Should I Include in My Blended Course?

As you start developing learning activities for a blended course, you may want to look at one or more of your previous courses to see the kinds of learning activities that you have used in the past. Using Table 5.3, list some of the different kinds of direct instruction and guided inquiry classes that you have most frequently used in your teaching or that you have found to be the most successful.

Once you have designed this list, consider whether these activities might work well in the blended course that you are designing, keeping in mind that some of the activities that you previously used in the face-to-face environment might need to be transitioned online. Looking at the direct instruction and guided inquiry activities that you listed, use the following reflective questions to help you to decide which of these learning activities might be a good fit for your course:

TABLE 5.3.
Previously Used Methods of Direct Instruction and Guided Inquiry

Direct Instruction	Guided Inquiry
(primarily instructor-led learning where students depend on the instructor for information or instructions to move forward)	(primarily student-led learning where students autonomously explore course materials with only minimal instructions or direction from the instructor)

BOX 5.7
Examples of Active Learning Activities

- Case studies
- Field trips
- Games
- Jigsaw activities (a form of small group, peer-led teaching)
- Large-group discussion
- Peer review
- Problem sets (individual, small group, or large group)
- Role-playing
- Self-assessment
- Short writing assignments
- Simulations
- Small group work or discussion
- Think/Pair/Share (students reflect independently, share their thoughts with a peer, and then share their peer discussions out to the large group)
    (Additional assessment learning activity examples are offered in Chapter 3.)

- Will any of these learning activities support the intended outcomes and assessments that I have created for the course?

Once you have decided whether any of your previous learning activities fit with your intended outcomes and assignments, you can use the following questions to brainstorm whether there are additional activities that you might want to add into your course. Although certainly not exhaustive, Box 5.7 also offers some examples of potential learning activities.

- What learning activities might encourage students to utilize technology for the purpose of enhancing their learning?

- What learning activities will work best with face-to-face interaction in order to effectively help students learn?

- Will group work help my students to learn the course materials and meet the objectives for the course?

When designing your blended course learning activities, you will want to consider the role of your face-to-face classroom.
Ask yourself the following:

- What kinds of face-to-face learning activities will help students learn best when I am physically present?

- What kinds of online learning activities will support student learning when I am not physically present (e.g., see Box 5.8)?

BOX 5.8
Best Practice Tip

McTighe and Wiggins (2004) offer the following suggestions for what should be homework or out-of-class activities:

- Practicing skills
- Reading with a purpose
- Working on project or performance task
- Studying and synthesizing information (e.g., create a concept map)
- Reflecting on ideas, process, or product (e.g., journal entry)
- Revising work

The reflective questions provided here are meant to help you compile a list of potential learning activities for your course that will support the intended outcomes and assessments. In addition to the intended outcomes and assessments already designed for your course, the answers to these questions will be dependent, at least in part, on the kinds of students enrolled in your course as well as the content of your course. Chapter 6 will offer tools and suggestions to help you map out these activities so that you can align them with your intended outcomes, assessments, and other learning activities as well as place them in an appropriate sequence.

Which of the Activities That I Have Chosen Should Be Face-to-Face and Which Should Be Online?

Now that you have a list of potential activities for your blended course, you will want to consider whether those activities should be offered face-to-face, online, or both. The checklist in Table 5.4 can help you decide whether your face-to-face activities should remain in the classroom or whether they should be moved online.

Once you have completed the checklist in Table 5.4, use Table 5.5 to categorize your list of learning activities as being face-to-face, online, or in both modalities.

As you decide where each of your learning activities belongs, you will also want to consider the amount of time that you have to transition face-to-face activities to the online environment, the online tools that are available for your course (see Chapter 7 and Chapter 11), your comfort level with various online tools, and the kinds of instructions or support that students will need to successfully complete online learning activities that you design (see Chapter 13).

Key Ideas From Chapter 5

- Active learning approaches are a successful, evidence-based practice for student learning.
- A "flipped" classroom is when content delivery is offered through the online components of a course so that more active learning can take place in the face-to-face classroom.

TABLE 5.4.
Blended Course Learning Activities Checklist

	Yes	No	Comments
Is there a particular reason to move this particular face-to-face learning activity online?	☐	☐	
Is there a limitation to this face-to-face learning activity that would be fixed by moving it online?	☐	☐	
Are there certain components of this learning activity that would benefit from being placed online?	☐	☐	
Will moving this learning activity online save additional class time for other important learning activities?	☐	☐	
Will moving this face-to-face activity online improve the learning experience for my students?	☐	☐	
Is it possible for me to transition this learning activity online and maintain the student learning experience of the original face-to-face version?	☐	☐	
Do I have the resources and/or tools to place this learning activity online? (See Chapter 7 for more information about specific online tools for your blended course.)	☐	☐	
Can my students complete this learning activity independently or with minimal support if it is placed online?	☐	☐	
Will my students have the resources or skills to complete this learning activity independently or with minimal support if it is placed online?	☐	☐	

TABLE 5.5.
Categorizing Learning Activities as Face-to-Face, Online, or Both

Face-to-Face	Online	Both Face-to-Face and Online

- In a blended course design, instructors should attempt to balance direct instruction and guided inquiry learning activities.
- All learning activities should be aligned with the intended outcomes and assessments for a blended course.
- Instructors should carefully consider whether the learning activities they choose for their blended course should be face-to-face, online, or both.

Questions for Faculty

- How familiar were you with the active learning approach before reading this chapter?
- What experiences have you had, both positive and negative, with active learning methods?
- Have you ever tried the flipped classroom model? What were some of the pros and cons of that experience?

Questions for Administrators

- Do you have resources available on your campus to help faculty increase their use of active learning methods in face-to-face and online environments (e.g., a teaching and learning library, a Center for Teaching and Learning, or an Academic Technology unit)?
- Are there policies or reward structures on your campus that support the use of active learning methods in face-to-face and online environments?

Documenting Your Course Design Progress

TABLE 5.6.
Documenting Your Course Design Progress

Course Design Steps	In Your LMS Sandbox
<ul><li>Use Table 5.3 to list the direct instruction and guided inquiry activities you have previously used.</li><li>Answer the reflective questions provided throughout the chapter to identify additional learning activities to include in your course.</li><li>Use Table 5.4 and Table 5.5 to categorize your learning activities as face-to-face, online, or both.</li></ul>	<ul><li>Create a list of the online learning activities you have identified in this chapter that will need to be incorporated into your LMS sandbox (this list can be reviewed when you read Chapter 7).</li></ul>

NOTES

6

MAPPING YOUR BLENDED COURSE

What Do We Know About Mapping Your Blended Course?

The process of course mapping is an integral component to creating a student-centered blended course design. Course mapping will help you to ensure that your blended course includes aligned goals, objectives, assessments, and learning activities in both your face-to-face and online environments so that students have a clear path of what they are learning and how to succeed in the course (see Table 6.1).

As Blumberg (2009) argues, "well-stated objectives can improve communication between instructors and students. They can make student learning more efficient and reduce student anxiety because they know what the instructor expects of them and what their learning priorities should be" (p. 96). For students who are new to the autonomous and independent learning environment of a blended course, clear objectives that are aligned with course assessments and activities can provide a roadmap to their success.

Along with student-centered design, the concept of constructive alignment (Biggs, 1996) provides a helpful framework for the course mapping activities presented later in this chapter. Coined by John Biggs, *constructive alignment* is a design process through which an instructor chooses particular course activities and designs assessments so that they are directly connected to, and in support of, pre-identified student learning objectives. This alignment creates a classroom environment where "learners arrive at meaning by actively selecting, and cumulatively constructing, their own knowledge, through both individual and social activity" (Biggs, 1996, p. 348). Biggs points to the importance of choosing learning objectives that are sufficiently challenging for students, designing activities that are meant to elicit a performance that provides evidence of student learning at a specific cognitive level, and creating assessments that can then evaluate whether students were able to accomplish the course objectives (e.g., see Box 6.1). Blended course designs based on constructive alignment have been shown to result in "significantly increased student interaction, engagement with learning and assessment tasks, and achievement of higher order outcomes" (Reaburn, Muldoon, & Bookallil, 2009, p. 829).

In the design of a traditional course, a constructive alignment mapping process can resemble a slightly more advanced version of the course schedule one might include in a syllabus (see Table 6.2).

TABLE 6.1.
Course Mapping Terminology Definitions

Intended Outcomes	What must students know and understand? What must students be able to do?
Assessments	What evidence will students provide of their learning?
Learning Activities	What activities and assignments will support the intended outcomes and assessments?

BOX 6.1
Relationship Between Intended Outcome and Assessment Example

If one learning objective of a course is for students to be able to *apply* the scientific method to a lab experiment, then an instructor may ask students to write up a lab report that offers a step-by-step explanation of the student's process in completing an experiment. When assessing this objective, the instructor might ask whether a student correctly included all of the steps, and *at what level of competence* they executed the components of the scientific method.

TABLE 6.2.
Traditional Course Design Alignment Map

Week	Topic/Content	Goal(s)	Learning Objective(s)	Assessment(s)	Learning Activities
1					
2					

Blended courses, however, include several additional components that need to be intentionally mapped to ensure student learning and success. In the step-by-step guide that follows, I offer descriptions of the different components that should be included in your blended course map, some examples of blended course maps, templates for weekly course mapping, and some guiding questions for course mapping that will help you self-assess your map as you create the structure for your course.

A Step-by-Step Guide to Mapping Your Blended Course

Components of Your Course Map

Week and Topic
Clearly mark each week, including the dates of face-to-face (F2F) meetings, and the topics or guiding questions for that week.

Objectives (F2F and Online)
For each week, outline the learning objectives that you want students to focus on in both the F2F and online activities for the course.

Direct Instruction (F2F and Online)
Note on your course map the times where students will receive direct instruction from you in the form of a F2F lecture, a video lecture, a video tutorial, or other medium where students will depend on you for information or instructions to move forward.

Guided Inquiry (F2F and Online)
Note on your course map the times where students will engage in guided inquiry, or primarily student-led learning activities, where students will autonomously explore course materials with only minimal instructions from the instructor. For example, online activities might include students watching a video clip of a documentary while answering guiding questions or interacting with one another on a discussion board. Examples of F2F guided inquiry might include research tasks, small group work, or other activities that students will complete mostly independently.

Social Presence (F2F and Online)
Note on your course map when students will be asked to intentionally engage in activities that ask them to communicate with you or their peers. This is called *social presence* and it is a component of blended course design that must be included very intentionally because it is often instinctual in F2F classrooms. (This component is discussed more explicitly in Chapter 8.)

Assessment/Evaluation (F2F and Online)
Include all formal and informal assessments and evaluations in your course map. You will want to note the tests, exams, quizzes, or other assignments that occur in the course and clearly mark whether they will happen in the F2F or online environment.

Metacognition/Reflection (F2F and Online)
Lastly, but certainly not least, make sure to note times when you are asking students to intentionally reflect on their own learning. In many courses, this can be an unplanned occurrence, but reflective activities are crucial for students who may be

BOX 6.2
Course Design Recommendation

For the template offered in Table 6.3, it can be helpful to transfer the template to a large sheet of poster paper and use Post-it notes to write in the different elements. This will allow components of the course to be easily moved and changed as you work toward a final version of the course map.

TABLE 6.3.
Template for Aligned Blended Course Mapping

Week & Topic	Goal (F2F & Online)	Objectives (F2F & Online)	Direct Instruction Learning Activities (F2F & Online)	Guided Inquiry Learning Activities (F2F & Online)	Social Presence Learning Activities (F2F & Online)	Assessment/ Evaluation (F2F & Online)	Metacognition/ Reflection (F2F & Online)

TABLE 6.4.
Template for Weekly Blended Course Mapping

Week _____		
Learning Objectives	*Online Modules*	*Online Checkpoints (Assessments)*
	F2F Activities	*F2F Checkpoints (Assessments)*
Notes on Content:		

experiencing a blended learning environment for the first time. By asking students to reflect on what is helping or hindering their learning in your course, you can also identify patterns and make adjustments to help students succeed.

Tables 6.3 and 6.4 offer templates for mapping out your blended course over the semester and week by week. See Box 6.2 for a best practice tip regarding these templates. These templates will allow you the flexibility of easily moving around course components and playing with different organizational structures until you find the right structure for all the elements. Tables 6.5 and 6.6 offer completed examples of Tables 6.3 and 6.4.

Questions to Consider While Course Mapping

As you begin to map out your course, keep the following questions in mind:

1. Should your learning objectives be scaffolded (i.e., do certain ones need to come before others)?

TABLE 6.5.

Partially Completed Template for Aligned Blended Course Mapping

Week & Topic	Goal	Objectives	Direct Instruction Learning Activities	Guided Inquiry Learning Activities	Social Presence Learning Activities	Assessment / Evaluation	Metacognition/ Reflection
Week 1: Introductions (some things to be completed before coming to the first face-to-face class)	Students will have an understanding of the overall course content, structure, and what they are expected to learn	Students will be able to navigate the LMS site (online), begin to meet one another, and successfully complete a syllabus quiz (online)	Students will view a demonstration video (online) that guides them through the LMS site and shows the major components of the course	Students will complete an initial reading with guiding questions (online) and an F2F independent activity to meet peers	Students will complete an introductory discussion board assignment to introduce themselves to one another (online)	Syllabus quiz (online) and pre-survey (F2F) to provide more information about what they already know about course topics	The pre-survey will include reflective questions about how each student prefers to learn

TABLE 6.6.
Example of Completed Template for Weekly Blended Course Mapping

Week 1: Introductions		
Learning Objectives	*Online Modules*	*Online Checkpoints (Assessments)*
Students will be able to navigate the LMS site (online), begin to meet one another, and successfully complete a syllabus quiz (online).	Video tutorial of LMS site	Syllabus quiz
	F2F Activities	*F2F Checkpoints (Assessments)*
	Icebreaker introductions activity and large group discussion of reading	Pre-survey
Notes on Content: The first reading for the course includes some important terminology. How can I best assess students' understanding of that terminology? Maybe through a discussion board posting?		

2. Do certain learning objectives repeat in multiple weeks (e.g., as students work on a larger assignment or project)?

3. What kind of assignment, activity or assessment might work best to help students accomplish a particular learning objective?

After you have finished a draft of your course map, consider the following:

1. How do the assessments in the course connect back to course goals?

2. How accurately do the assessments measure student achievement of learning objectives?

3. Are there any learning objectives that are not measured in the course assessments?

4. Is there a mix of both instructor-led teaching (direct instruction) and student-centered learning (guided inquiry)?

5. Do you provide students with both F2F and online opportunities for direct instruction and guided inquiry?

6. Do you provide students with both F2F and online opportunities for assessing if they are achieving the course's learning objectives?

7. Do you create a strong sense of social presence of yourself and your students? (For more on social presence, see Chapter 8.)

Transitioning Your Course Map to a Syllabus Schedule

Once you have a course map that you are comfortable with, you will want to use components of the map to communicate to students the structure and schedule for your course. There may be parts of the course map that you want to keep to yourself for your own teaching notes. Tables 6.7 and 6.8 offer two examples of blended course schedules that were included in a syllabus and shared with students. One important thing to note is how the instructors clarify which components of the course are F2F and which are meant to occur online. (Additional information about preparing your blended syllabus is included in Chapter 12.)

TABLE 6.7.
Example One of Blended Course Map

Legend for schedule:

F2F = Face-to-face meeting agenda: Keep track of your section's meeting time

M = Instructional module: Complete the modules and any readings before your F2F meeting

P = Project: The fieldwork for these assignments is scheduled during those weeks

D = Discussion/response readings: 500-word responses are due by class time on the day that you are to discuss the article

Week	Topic	Out-of-Class Work	F2F Meeting	What's Due
0	Getting acclimated to working online	M0: Pre-class orientation to online resources		Print syllabus, make online profile
1	From natural philosophy to biology	M1: Evolution before Darwin M2: Earth history	Course welcome and overview	
2	Phylogenies	M3: Working with fossils M4: The tree of life D1: Derry 1999	Science as a process	Response 1
3	Variation	P1: The comparative method (@ MCZ) M5: Cellular basis of variation	Building evolutionary trees	

Reproduced with permission from Eric Dewar.

TABLE 6.8.
Example Two of Blended Course Map

Date	Assignment
Week 1: 1/15, Tues	**First in-class meeting:** Prior to class, complete two tasks outlined on Blackboard's Announcement Page

Week 2:
Prior to 1/22, Tues
	Read Chapter 1: Statistics and Data
	    1.1 The Relevance of Statistics
	    1.2 What is Statistics?
	    1.3 Variables and Scales of Measurement
	Watch Module 1. Statistics and Data [linked]
	Complete LearnSmart Chapter 1

1/22, Tues	**Read** Chapter 2: Tabular and Graphical Methods
	    2.1 Summarizing Qualitative Data
	    2.2 Summarizing Quantitative Data
	Watch Module 2. Tabular and Graphical Methods [linked]
	Complete LearnSmart Chapter 2

1/24, Thurs	**In-class meeting** on Chapter 1: Sections 1.1–1.3 and Chapter 2: Sections 2.1–2.2 **Submit** Homework Assignment 1 and Homework Assignment 2 by 10 a.m.

Week 3:
Prior to 1/29, Tues
	Read Chapter 3: Numerical Descriptive Measures
	    3.1 Measures of Central Location
	    3.2 Percentiles and Boxplots
	    3.4 Measures of Dispersion
	    3.6 Chebshev's Theorem and the Empirical Rule
	    3.7 Summarizing Grouped Data
	Watch Module 3. Numerical Descriptive Measures [linked]
	Complete LearnSmart Chapter 3

1/29, Tues 1/31, Thurs	**In-class meeting** on Chapter 3: Sections 3.1–3.2, 3.4, 3.6–3.7. **Submit** Homework Assignment 3 by 10 a.m.

Reproduced with permission from Alison Kelly.

Key Ideas From Chapter 6

- Course mapping is a process that should be learning centered.
- Constructivist alignment can help you ensure that your learning objectives are connected to your course activities, assignments, and assessments.
- A good course map can help students who are new to the blended learning environment navigate the course and succeed as learners.
- Not all of the elements of your course map will be included in your syllabus; you can decide what components are for your planning and organization and which will be shared with students.

Questions for Faculty

- What kind of course mapping have you completed for traditional courses that you have taught?
- What components of the blended course mapping described in this chapter are similar to or different from this previous experience?
- If you have taught blended courses in the past, are there additional components that you have included in your course map to help students navigate the course?

Questions for Administrators

- What support does your institution have in place to help faculty engage in a blended course mapping process (faculty development office, teaching and learning center, online resources, syllabus template, model examples, etc.)?
- Are there particular components of a blended course map that should be a mandatory requirement in blended course syllabi?

Documenting Your Course Design Progress

TABLE 6.9.
Documenting Your Course Design Progress

Course Design Steps	In Your LMS Sandbox
• Locate all holidays, exams, and other important dates and count the weeks and course days available in the term that you will be teaching your blended course. • Begin to fill out the blended course map template in Table 6.3 with the elements of your course that you have already planned and keep the course map handy for when you need to add additional components after completing future workbook chapters. • Complete the reflective questions to consider while course mapping to help self-assess the course map as you create it. • Consider which elements of your course map you might want to include in your syllabus schedule (this will help you prepare for Chapter 12).	• Find out if your LMS has a calendar tool and decide whether you plan to use it within your course to help students remember due dates and deadlines. • Wait until your course map is complete and solidified before building your LMS site structure; it may be difficult to make changes throughout the site later on if you move assignments to another week or rearrange learning objectives.

NOTES

7

GETTING TO KNOW YOUR LEARNING MANAGEMENT SYSTEM

With Sarah Smith

What Do We Know About Learning Management Systems?

One of the key components of your blended course is the delivery of the online portion. A popular choice for higher education institutions is the LMS and your campus may even have a policy of which platform is used to host online content (see Box 7.1).

Many institutions have invested in one LMS for their campus. Commonly used LMSs include:

- Blackboard Learn (www.blackboard.com/learning-management-system/blackboard-learn.aspx)
- Canvas (www.canvaslms.com)
- Desire2Learn (www.brightspace.com)
- Moodle (https://moodle.org)

Some of these platforms offer a free educator option if you want to try out the LMS or if you need a sandbox space to start designing a course.

LMSs can offer a variety of tools to help instructors communicate with students, organize course content, and assess student learning (more on these tools later in the chapter), but scholars have been careful to point out that an LMS does not have a built-in pedagogy (Carmean & Brown, 2005). It is the instructor's intentional integration of LMS tools for online learning that can help an LMS cater to a diverse range of student learning styles and a range of student ability levels (Vovides, Sanchez-Alonso, Mitropoulou, & Nickmans, 2007; Koszalka & Ganesan, 2010). Studies have also illustrated that in a blended environment, intentional LMS tool integration can help students to better manage and self-regulate their learning (Kilmon & Fagan, 2007; O'Brien, Campbell, & Earp, 2005; Vovides et al., 2007).

Instructors typically underutilize the LMS when they limit themselves to only posting a syllabus or other content without using any of the other tools available (Carmean & Brown, 2005; Vovides et al., 2007). As LMSs gain more popularity, the

BOX 7.1
What Is an LMS?

An LMS (sometimes also called "Course Management System" or "E-Learning Platform") is a software system that offers an organization structure for a range of online course tools to be used by both groups and individuals. LMSs typically include a suite of tools designed to deliver, track, report on, and manage learning content, student progress, and student-instructor interactions.

literature provides evidence that merely posting information on a course website does not help students learn. For example, in a recent study, Kember, McNaught, Chong, Lam, and Cheng (2010) found that "dialogic interactivity involving interaction with content resources (e.g., with quizzes, simulations, games, interactive tutorials, etc.) and with people (e.g., with peer learners and teachers in forums, online role plays, wikis, blogs, etc.) appears to be more effective" (p. 1191) than merely having access to course information and documents.

As you design your blended course, it is important to explore the range of tools included in your LMS and to choose the tools that will best help your students learn. Kilmon and Fagan (2007) found that successfully utilizing an LMS requires "advance planning, good organizational skills, more attention to details, and improved written communication skills" (p. 141). In the remainder of the chapter, we outline the basic tools included in LMS software, provide a series of activities that you can use to decide which tools are best to integrate into your course, and provide a list of questions to help you learn more about the LMS on your campus. Throughout the chapter, we have also integrated best practices for designing a course in an LMS environment.

LMS Features

LMSs have a variety of features and it is important to decide which features will be the most helpful for the students in your blended course to learn the material specific to your discipline. (For more on assessment-related features in your LMS, see Chapter 4.)

Typical tools of LMS software include the following:

File Organization

Most LMSs have space for instructors to upload files such as readings, a syllabus, course assignments, and other relevant course documents. A best practice with designing a course within an LMS is to think carefully about file organization. Instructors should consider using folders to organize readings or other files by date to be accessed, topic, or another categorization to ensure that all course materials are easy to find.

Communication Tools

There are two different kinds of communication tools included in most LMS features. Synchronous tools encourage student engagement with the instructor and student peers in real time. Asynchronous tools allow for students to respond to questions or comments from the instructor or their peers over a longer time period. The following are examples of each kind of tool. When choosing communication tools for a blended learning environment, instructors should consider the kinds of skills they are asking students to practice and demonstrate, as well as the kinds of thinking most appropriate for the disciplinary content. Many blended courses take advantage of synchronous and asynchronous communication tools to keep students engaged in learning in between face-to-face classroom meetings.

- Synchronous tools: chat rooms, virtual meeting spaces (also called online classrooms or web conferencing), wikis
- Asynchronous tools: discussion boards, blogs, wikis, emails, announcements, journals

Collaborative Tools

To help students collaborate with one another outside of face-to-face classroom meetings, instructors in blended classrooms can utilize online tools such as wikis, shared documents, private group spaces, as well as some of the communication tools listed previously. When collaborative tools are integrated into a blended course, instructors need to help students navigate the expectations for group work using these tools. Face-to-face discussions about expectations can help prepare student for experiences with online group work.

Time Management Tools

Many LMSs offer tools to help students organize their assignments and effectively manage their time. Instructors can set up a calendar of important dates, a notification system to remind students of upcoming deadlines, as well as a task list so students can map their progress throughout a course.

Lesson Planning Tools

A helpful feature for blended courses are the lesson planning tools that can assist instructors to create learning modules to chunk material. Lesson Plans partner curricular resources, such as learning objectives, subject area, and instructional level with the lesson. Learning Modules are a slightly different tool that offer instructors the opportunity to guide students' interaction with course materials in a digital environment. Learning Modules can group course files, assignments, quizzes, and other activities in an instructor defined order all in one place for ease of use by students.

Media Integration

For instructors who wish to include video and audio files in their courses, some LMSs allow for integration of media sites such as YouTube. If you plan to include video lectures with your course, we recommend talking with your technology department about the tools that your institution may support. You may also want to discuss any media you choose to use with your institution's disability service office to make sure

BOX 7.2
Best Practice Tip

Don't do too much too fast. Try a couple new tools at a time so that you don't overwhelm yourself or your students. Using one or two new tools in your blended course will also make it easier to assess whether or not the tools are helping your students learn.

that all media is accessible for students with disabilities. (This topic is explored in more depth in Chapter 10.)

Usually LMSs are private learning spaces that require students to have a login and password to view and interact with course materials. Once a course has been created within an LMS, however, instructors often have the option of recycling materials through a copy or export feature if the course is repeated with a new group of students. For long-term storage, courses created in an LMS can frequently be archived by the instructor. Since policies are different at every institution, we recommend you check with the appropriate technology department on your campus to see if courses hosted in the LMS are deleted after a certain period.

A Step-by-Step Guide to Learning About Your LMS

Depending on the kinds of skills you want students to demonstrate upon completion of your course, you will want to choose LMS tools appropriate for your outcomes. (See Box 7.2 for a best practice tip regarding choosing new tools.)

Using Tools to Measure Student Learning Objectives

1. What do your course goals and learning objectives (from Chapter 2) include in terms of skills that you want your students to demonstrate?

2. Are there LMS tools that would help you measure your students' mastery of these skills?

3. Are there any LMS tools that you have used before that would help your students meet the course goals and learning objectives?

4. Are there any LMS tools that you have wanted to try that would help your students meet the course goals and learning objectives?

Table 7.1 offers some suggestions for LMS tools that align with particular andragogies and course designs. Table 7.2 offers an LMS tools checklist that you can use once you have made some initial decisions about the tools you might want to implement in your blended course.

One of the first things your students will see in your LMS course is the menu that is prominently displayed. Choosing how to organize this menu and what to include to help students navigate your course is one of the first steps of designing your LMS site. (See Box 7.3 for a best practice tip.)

Standard menu options include:

- Announcements
- Syllabus
- Course Content/Readings
- Assignments
- Discussion Board
- Contact Your Instructor
- Help Features (institutional support resources including IT help desk, disability services, student learning/tutoring office, etc.)

In Table 7.3 we have offered some menu examples with different organizational structures for all of your course materials.

In addition to the organizational structure of your course materials, it is also important to think about how best to organize the actual online content of your

---

BOX 7.3
Best Practice Tip

We recommend that you conform to "common sense" naming conventions, so students do not struggle to find the various components of your blended course. Some standard menu options are included in this chapter for guidance.

TABLE 7.1.
LMS Course Tools Taxonomy

Discussion-Based Course	*Teamwork-Based Course*	*Reflection-Based Course*
Discussion board	Wiki	Journal
Blogs	Private group spaces	Email
Chat	Discussion board	Discussion board
Virtual classroom	Shared documents	Blogs
	Virtual classroom	

TABLE 7.2.
Choosing LMS Tools Checklist

	Yes	*No*	*Comments*
Does the LMS tool fit with my learning objectives for the course?	☐	☐	
Does the LMS tool promote active learning?	☐	☐	
Does the LMS tool help me to assess my students' learning?	☐	☐	
Is the LMS tool accessible for all students?	☐	☐	
Is the LMS tool easy for students to find and navigate?	☐	☐	
Does the LMS tool include clear instructions for students (if applicable)?	☐	☐	
Do I need to create any supplemental materials to help students learn through this LMS tool?	☐	☐	
Would this LMS tool work better if paired with another LMS tool or online resource?	☐	☐	
Is this the best LMS tool I can find to help my students learn this material?	☐	☐	

course (readings, multimedia content, web resources) in order to help your students learn. In the next activity, we offer some guided questions to help you think more specifically about your content organization. Box 7.4 also offers some ideas for different ways to organize content.

BOX 7.4
Ways to Organize Content

- How students learn
- Week-to-week
- Every class period
- Learning modules
- Themes
- Topics

TABLE 7.3.
Example LMS Menu Structures

Common Course Menu	Course Menu Structured by Date of Access	Course Menu Structured by Unit
Getting Started	Announcements	Announcements
Announcements	Syllabus	Syllabus
Syllabus	Week 1—Face-to-Face	Unit 1—Sept 4
Course Content	Week 2—Online	Unit 2—Sept 11
Assignments	Week 3—Face-to-Face	Unit 3—Sept 18
Discussions	Week 4—Online	Unit 4—Sept 25
Contact Instructor	Contact Instructor	Contact Instructor
Grade Book	Grade Book	Grade Book
24-Hour LMS Support	24-Hour LMS Support	24-Hour LMS Support

Questions on Organizing Course Content

1. How is content usually structured in your face-to-face course? Why is content structured this way?

2. What are the benefits and/or limitations of this typical structure of course content? Does that structure fit your blended course?

3. Are there disciplinary reasons to organize your content in a particular way? (For example, are you teaching a course with a lab component?)

BOX 7.5
Best Practice Tip

Try to stick to the "three-click rule" so that students can find the components of your blended course in three clicks or less. If content for your course is too embedded, students may get confused trying to find it.

TABLE 7.4.
Example One of LMS Content Area

Area: <u>Syllabus and Welcome</u>	
Folders	*Documents/Learning Modules/Tools*
🗁 Syllabus Documents	📄 Syllabus 📄 List of Course Readings Linked in the LMS
🗁 Week 1 Introductions	📄 Link to Welcome Message on Announcements Page 📄 Link to Week 1 Discussion Board Introduction Activity

TABLE 7.5.
Example Two of LMS Content Area

Area: <u>Course Content</u>	
Folders	*Documents/Learning Modules/Tools*
🗁 Week 1	📄 Reading 📄 Link to Quiz in LMS
🗁 Week 2	📄 Learning Module 1 (includes quiz) 📄 Supplementary Reading
🗁 Week 3	📄 Learning Module 2 (includes quiz) 📄 Supplementary Reading
🗁 Week 4	📄 Study Guide for Test 1 📄 Link to Discussion Board to post questions for Test 1

When structuring your course, you want to consider the audience and make sure your blended course design is intuitive to students who will not be familiar with your content. (See Box 7.5 for a best practice tip.) Students entering your LMS course may already be exploring the web and are familiar with using only a few clicks to reach

TABLE 7.6.
Template for Mapping Content and Documents

Area: _____	
Folders	*Documents/Learning Modules/Tool Links*
📁	📄
	📄

Area: _____	
Folders	*Documents/Learning Modules/Tool Links*
📁	📄
	📄
📁	📄
	📄

Area: _____	
Folders	*Documents/Learning Modules/Tool Links*
📁	📄
	📄
📁	📄
	📄

what they need. Give your students a design they already know how to operate so they can concentrate on their learning.

Tables 7.4 and 7.5 offer some examples and Table 7.6 offers a template for mapping out your content areas with the documents, tools, and activities that will make up your course.

Once you have chosen the tools you plan to use, organized your LMS menu, and chosen a structure for the content of your LMS, you will want to explore the aesthetic choices available within your LMS, including text color, "theme" options, and icon possibilities. Please note that you may have students with visual disabilities so you should plan to use text labels for content along with color. Take advantage of the text editor fields provided by your LMS and include information beyond file names. Most LMSs allow the instructor to select menu styles with a range of colors for text or buttons.

Assessing the Quality of Your LMS Design

Although your campus may have professionals who can help assess the quality of your blended course design within an LMS, another option is Quality Matters© (QM).

QM offers a detailed rubric with eight standards to guide assessment of the quality of online and blended courses. The QM rubric is based on research literature regarding online and blended learning and the rubric is learning-centered. According to QM, "the review process is intended to be diagnostic and collegial, not evaluative and judgmental" (Quality Matters, 2016). Visit www.QMprogram.org for more information on QM.

Some LMS companies also provide guidance on best design practices. For example, Blackboard Learn has created the Exemplary Course Program Rubric available online. This tool allows instructors and course designers to evaluate how well a course conforms to best practices for course design, interaction and collaboration, assessment, and learner support. Furthermore, you can adopt the evaluation criteria to make an exemplary course. Review the rubric online (www.blackboard.com/resources/catalyst-awards/BbExemplaryCourseRubric_Nov2013.pdf) to identify your course design and prioritize changes through a self-evaluation.

Key Ideas From Chapter 7

- LMSs have a variety of tools that can enhance the blended classroom.
- To ensure effective student learning, instructors should intentionally choose LMS tools that are connected to their intended course outcomes.
- The design of a course structured through an LMS can help or hinder learning; instructors should intentionally and purposefully choose their LMS organizational structures.
- Because of institutional differences, instructors should familiarize themselves with the LMS on their campus, its features, and support mechanisms to receive training on LMS tools as well as help with LMS course design and set-up.
- Online rubrics, such as the one provided by QM, can help instructors gauge the effectiveness of the online learning structure they create within an LMS.

Questions for Faculty

- What LMS does your institution use?
- Does your institution have any basic requirements for faculty use of the LMS (i.e., does everyone have to post their course syllabus online)?
- Are regular trainings offered on LMS features?
- Are you able to have an LMS space (i.e., a sandbox) to try out different tools and features without actually running out a course?
- Does your institutional LMS have any special features?
- Are courses created in an LMS deleted after a certain time period?
- Does your institution have an Office of Disability Services, and have they checked your LMS to see if it is accessible for all learners, particularly those with sensory disabilities?

Questions for Administrators

- Does your institution have a policy about how faculty members use the LMS system for traditional, blended, or online courses?
- Does your institution have any basic requirements for faculty use of the LMS (i.e., does everyone have to post their course syllabus online)?
- What is your institution's long-term plan for your current LMS? Do you plan to continue to use the same product, or are you exploring different options based on faculty and student needs?
- Who supports the LMS at your institution? Does that person or office gather feedback from faculty and students about their use of the LMS?
- Does your institution have an Office of Disability Services, and have you created an institutional policy to have this office review blended courses before they are launched to ensure they are accessible for all learners, particularly those with sensory disabilities?
- Do you have an institutional structure through which you can discuss technology tool integration, e-policies, and the evaluation of online courses with department heads, IT professionals, and other institutional stakeholders?

Documenting Your Course Design Progress

TABLE 7.7.
Documenting Your Course Design Progress

Course Design Steps	*In Your LMS Sandbox*
• Choose which LMS components you plan to include in your blended course. • Use Table 7.6 to map out the content areas for your LMS site. • Find out if there are best practice design resources for your LMS; these resources might be institution-specific or through your LMS provider. • Review the work you have completed for previous chapters to see what might pertain to what you have learned in this chapter regarding your LMS.	• Decide the structure for your LMS navigation menu. • Based on the map you created in Table 7.6, begin to create the content areas for your blended course on the LMS site. • Explore the aesthetic choices available within your LMS including text color, "theme" options, and icon possibilities. • Review the work you have completed for previous chapters to see what you can add into your LMS site given what you have learned in this chapter.

NOTES

8

CREATING SOCIAL PRESENCE
IN YOUR BLENDED COURSE

With Victoria Wallace

What Do We Know About Creating Social Presence in Your Blended Course?

Creating an environment that is conducive to learning is important in any course that an instructor designs. For online and blended courses, the concept of social presence contributes to a successful learning environment (see Box 8.1). Also called "being there" (Lehman & Conceição, 2010, p. vii), social presence helps students to effectively engage with you and one another when communicating online. While this kind of communication happens fairly automatically in a face-to-face class (e.g., your physical presence in the room can serve to influence and motivate students), in a blended modality it must be intentionally built into the course design. In the face-to-face classroom, you are able to read body language, facilitate discussions on the fly, identify and engage learners who are timid, and keep discussions productive. Moving to a blended course design will require a shift in how you connect with your students.

Fortunately, you may already be planning to implement online tools that will help your students experience the concept of social presence. LMS components such as discussion boards, chat features, and web conferencing are all examples of tools that can enhance social presence while learning online. Moreover, Lehman and Conceição (2010) argue that social presence begins when the instructor "has placed the learner in the center of the course development and created the course for that learner" (p. 3); thus, the work that you have already done throughout this book has gotten you off to a good start!

When planning to integrate components of social presence into your course, intimacy and immediacy are two important factors to consider. The research suggests that addressing each student's individual needs and characteristics in a timely manner positively impacts the perception of social presence more so than communication medium or design (Gunawardena, 1995; Kelley & Gorham, 1988; Shea, 2006; So & Brush, 2008). In part, this means helping a student to feel present and known in the online environment. Garrison (2011) defines *social presence* as a fairly complex online tenet. Students must be able to identify with the group or course to some degree and feel they are participating in a trusting environment to communicate freely and purposely. This, in turn, allows students to exhibit personal characteristics, emotion, and

BOX 8.1
What Is Social Presence?

There is no formally agreed-upon definition of *social presence* across researchers. Generally, however, social presence is the inclusion of intentional activities and elements of the online environment that ask students to communicate and interact with the instructor or their peers.

feeling, and develop relationships and connect with their peers and the instructor. All of these aspects are associated with social presence.

A subset of the research on social presence is focused on the impact of discussion boards, or asynchronous online discussion (AOD), on students' learning. In a study by Beckett, Amaro-Jimenez, and Beckett (2010), the authors found that graduate students used discussion boards as "virtual communities of practice for language socialization and as opportunities to learn the languages and cultures of the academic and professional communities that they were part of by engaging with more knowledgeable and experienced others" (p. 327). Kim (2011) and King and So (2014) found similar socialization and learning outcomes benefits for nonnative speakers of English who contributed to online discussion boards. There are also several other benefits that discussion boards and other aspects of social presence can offer for students in blended courses. Collison, Elbaum, Haavind, and Tinker (2000) note that discussion boards can "extend reflection time" and offer the "opportunity to compose thoughtful, probing contributions" (p. 2; see also, Meyer, 2003). They also point out that virtual discussions can allow students and the instructor to share links or resources in real time and also that online discussion forums "provide little place for 'disengaged' participants to hide or fake their involvement" (p. 2). Bender (2012) further articulates that "online discussion can reach beyond the temporal and spatial constraints of the campus class, and as a result can often add a richer and deeper perspective as students respond when they are informed and inspired" (p. 2). An additional benefit to any online discussion is that it can be recorded (whether in text-based, video, or audio formats) for later review by you or your students.

The Importance of Social Presence

Social presence is an important concept for the blended classroom because it has been shown to improve learning, interpersonal relationships, persistence, motivation, and satisfaction (Jusoff & Khodabandelou, 2009; Rovai, 2002; Tu, 2001). There is also evidence that social presence indirectly improves short-term memory, supports knowledge construction and meaning making, and enables critical thinking (Brookfield, 2012; Garrison, Anderson, & Archer, 2000; Kelley & Gorham, 1988). Elements of social presence can also impact community building and interpersonal relationships. Importantly, a sense of community has been found to be linked to perceived learning (Rovai, 2002). Shea (2006) found that students' sense of community (shared purpose, trust, and relationships) were positively related to an instructor's presence. Several scholars have also found that students' perceptions of social presence correlated with their perceptions of learning and satisfaction (Gunawardena & Zittle, 1997; Richardson & Swan, 2003). While there are many variables that contribute to students' success in a blended environment, current research provides evidence that instructors can positively impact the student experience by being socially present and creating an environment that supports social presence.

The Instructor's Role

The instructor plays a vital role in encouraging interaction in the online environment, possibly more so than the technology tools that are integrated or the course design model that is chosen by the instructor (Loncar, Barrett, & Liu, 2014). In the blended classroom, part of your role is to ensure the online portion of a blended course supports a trusting, open environment and provides for and encourages interaction among participants. To facilitate social presence, you should design a course that promotes connectedness and belonging through personalization and shared experiences. Palloff and Pratt (2007) posit six elements as critical to successful online communities:

1. *Honesty*: Communicate with your students respectfully and honestly. Safety and trust must be established so that students can feel comfortable sharing openly, honestly, and respectfully with you and their peers.
2. *Responsiveness*: Respond to students in a timely manner and model responsiveness. Students' responses and instructor feedback must happen in a timely manner so that interaction across and among students builds an acquisition of knowledge through which the community can grow.
3. *Relevance*: Encourage students to bring their life experiences and knowledge into the online classroom. Real-world examples and opportunities to share enhance the learning process for everyone.
4. *Respect*: Provide an environment where students feel respected as individuals and where they can grow and learn as a community. You can facilitate this by welcoming the group, providing constructive and thoughtful feedback, and giving students opportunities to make shared decisions about assignments, assessments, or other components of the course. You can also provide feedback and communication guidelines to your students or have groups create their own contract.
5. *Openness*: Design safe, low-stakes opportunities where students can post insights and experiences that do not align with mainstream understanding. Students should feel confident that feedback will be respectful and the experience will contribute to everyone's growth.
6. *Empowerment*: Create a learning environment where students are central to their own learning. Encourage learners to explore additional resources and share with the group. (pp. 228–231)

The Student's Role

In addition to paying attention to your own role as a facilitator of social presence, it is important to establish expectations for your students as well. For example, what are your expectations for the frequency of student engagement and what successful engagement looks like with online tools such as discussion board forums? When choosing elements of social presence to include in your blended course, you will want to remember that students may be familiar with using online tools for being social, but they may be less familiar with using these tools in a learning environment. Sharing your expectations will help acculturate your students to the online tools and help to set them up for success. Consider incorporating the following into your course:

Guidelines For Respectful Online Interaction

You can either provide guidelines for respectful online interaction, or ask your students to create these guidelines together during an in-class session early in the course. There are also several "netiquette" guides that you could post as a supplementary resource for students so that they are aware, for example, that typing in ALL CAPS constitutes shouting in an online environment.

Clear Instructions For All Online Social Tools

If you decide to implement discussion boards, chat features, or web conferencing tools, create instructions for students about what you expect their interaction to look like with these tools. For example, you will want to decide how many posts constitute "active" participation. Also, students will want to know with what frequency, and with what degree of formality, they should reference course materials or in-class conversations or activities when posting. You will also want to share what you expect regarding the length of a post and how often or how many times students should respond to one another. It is also important to clarify for students what you consider to be mandatory engagement for them online and what is optional.

Grading Rubrics For Online Participation

Once you have established the expectations for online engagement among your students, consider posting rubrics so that students will know how their participation will be evaluated in these environments. Social presence is an intentional component of the course and students should be aware of how they are expected to contribute using the different online tools that you make available.

A Step-by-Step Guide to Creating Social Presence in Your Blended Course

The concept of social presence might already be familiar to you because of activities that are included in your traditional courses. We recommend that you start planning for social presence in your blended classroom by first thinking about the activities that you already use to establish social presence in your traditional courses and considering how these activities or elements might translate to your blended environment. In Table 8.1, we have provided some examples of social presence in face-to-face classrooms that are translated for online environments to get you started.

TABLE 8.1.
Examples of Social Presence in Face-to-Face and Online Environments

Examples of Social Presence in Face-to-Face Classroom	Examples of Social Presence in Online Classroom
Facilitating a first-day icebreaker	Create a discussion board forum where you and your students can post introductions and photos
Creating a contact list of students	Use a wiki for students to post their names, photos, contact information, and scholarly interests
Conducting office hours	Use the chat feature in your LMS or synchronous tools like Adobe Connect or Google Hangouts to hold virtual office hours
Providing feedback	In addition to the other feedback mechanisms in your course, which should occur early and often, consider sending short podcasts to each learner to let them know how they are doing at midterm (see more about podcasts in Chapter 10)
Hosting Q&A sessions and exam reviews	Use synchronous tools like Adobe Connect or Google Hangouts to hold live Q&A and exam review sessions (you can record and archive the session in case some learners are unable to attend) or create a discussion board forum for students to post questions they have about the course or upcoming exams (this way all students can access your responses any time, and a record is created)

Tips for Improving Social Presence in Your Blended Course

It is important to include elements of social presence throughout an entire course. In this section, we offer some suggestions for components of social presence that can be implemented before a class begins, during the class, and after the class is completed. We have left blank spaces after each section so that you can also add your own ideas.

Before Class

- Create discussion prompts that allow students to voice their opinions, have respectful debates, contribute their perspectives, and share personal experiences.
- Set expectations early regarding communications. Provide guidelines on peer review, "netiquette," communications, and other elements that you think are important.
- Let students know how you will be participating in the online conversations (e.g., infrequently post but read daily and summarize weekly).
- Create an "off-topic/water cooler" online discussion area where students can exchange ideas not necessarily related to course topics.
- Establish a Facebook or Twitter group or page for your class (see Chapter 11 for more on using social media platforms in your course).

- Create opportunities where small groups can work toward a common goal to share with the class (e.g., build lists, a library of resources).

- _____

- _____

- _____

During Class

- Require students to post an introduction with a photo or avatar of themselves as the first class activity.
- Ask students to share their background and goals for the course.
- Require students to respond to their peers' posts with examples, references, personal experiences, success stories, or other feedback.
- Share your own personal stories and professional experiences related to course topics and materials.
- Summarize online discussions weekly to show you have been reading and synthesizing posts and appreciate students' engagement.
- Set up small groups for online discussions and activities. Select participants based on shared interests or other characteristics related to the course content.
- Have small groups choose a team name and develop a team charter at the beginning of the course.

- _____

- _____

- _____

End of Class

- Ask students to post a reflection of what they have learned and include three significant comments, observations, or moments for how their peers contributed to their learning.
- Keep the course Facebook group or website open and let students know they can continue to connect in this space.

- _____

- _____

- _____

Developing Successful Online Discussions

The discussion board feature in your LMS is an excellent tool for creating social presence in the online component of your blended course. Students can use this tool to connect asynchronously with one another, which can offer students, particularly those who need a little more time to process the course materials, the chance to collect their thoughts and articulate questions on their own timeline. Discussion board conversations can also be a great jumping-off point for in-class activities or discussions as well as a way for the instructor to note patterns of interest or confusion among the students in the course.

However, it is important to note that students may not have ever participated in a discussion board for the purpose of learning. As noted previously, outlining your expectations for their engagement with this tool and providing examples of a successful post will be important to your students' success. Also, making sure that you are actively engaged in the discussion boards will help students to recognize the forums as an important component of their participation in the course. Active discussion boards can become lengthy amounts of text, so you will also want to think about how you can ensure that students are reading regularly through the information that is posted so that they can keep up with the discussions. As noted previously, we recommend that you create weekly summaries of the discussions to help students understand the main points that arose across the forums. A good sign of a successful discussion board is multiple "layers" of responses to various posts. If you are seeing student posts that are not receiving any form of interaction from their peers (i.e., just staying at one layer), then there probably is not as much interaction occurring among your students as you might like. On the other hand, a post that elicits several responses, and then responses to those responses, indicates a lively online discussion. For students who may not have participated in a successful discussion board, you can model the kind of interaction you are looking for. Additionally, you can build the appropriate discussion board interactions into the assessment of students' posts, offering more credit when posts elicit a response from a peer, asks a good reflective question, or when students respond to their peers' posts in an engaged manner.

To ensure successful social presence opportunities and varied discussions, we also recommend including, at minimum, the following forums:

- *Introductions*: Create a forum for you and your students to introduce themselves to one another. Include some questions, as well as your own introduction as an example, to get the forum started. This low-stakes discussion forum will help acclimate students to the idea of posting online. Also, this discussion forum can act as an easy technology literacy test (see Chapter 13 for more on this) to implement before the course begins.
- *Technology Questions*: Create a space for students to post any issues they are having with the technology tools for the course. This will allow you to know if there are specific areas of concern that need troubleshooting or further explanation during the in-class sessions. It will also allow students to help one another with technology issues that arise.
- *Content Questions*: Create a space for students to ask questions about the course content. It is important to separate out the questions that students may have about what they are learning from the questions they might have about the course structure, technology tools, or other course logistics.

- *Course Feedback*: At the beginning of the course, or at midterm, open a discussion forum for students to offer feedback about the course and their learning. You can prompt students with questions like: What about the course is helping you learn? What about the course is making it more challenging for you to learn? What suggestions do you have to make the course better for you and your peers?

Key Ideas From Chapter 8

- While social presence can be an instinctual component of a traditional face-to-face class, instructors need to intentionally include components to encourage social presence when using online tools and platforms.
- Traditional elements of social presence can be translated for the online environment using asynchronous and synchronous tools.
- Discussion board forums can be an important element of social presence in your course, but students may need guidance to successfully use this online tool.
- It is important to establish clear expectations and guidelines for how students should interact with elements of social presence that you build into your blended course.

Questions for Faculty

- What kinds of methods will you use to connect with your students when you are not physically together?
- How will your students interact and build relationships with one another when they are not physically together in a classroom?
- In what consistent ways can you "be there" in the online components of your class?
- Have you established expectations for yourself about the frequency of communications you plan to have with students using online tools (e.g., how often you will check and respond to discussion board posts)?
- How will you manage these expectations with your students?

Questions for Administrators

- Does your institution have policies about the use of online tools external to your LMS for communication between faculty and students (e.g., the use of social media platforms in the classroom)?
- Are there opportunities on your campus where instructors can practice elements of social presence outside of the classroom experience (e.g., the use of web conferencing for meetings or webinars for professional development)?

Documenting Your Course Design Progress

TABLE 8.2.
Documenting Your Course Design Progress

Course Design Steps	In Your LMS Sandbox
• Add to your blended course map (started in Chapter 6) with the components of social presence that you plan to include in the course each week. • Establish expectations for yourself about the frequency of communications you plan to have with students using online tools. • Consider how to manage student expectations of your online social presence; is this something that you will discuss with them face-to-face or include in your syllabus?	• Add separate feedback discussion boards in your LMS to collect student questions about technology and content. • Add a discussion board in your LMS for students to introduce themselves to one another. • Create a space for students to have "off-topic" conversations.

NOTES

9

FINDING RESOURCES ONLINE

What Do We Know About Finding Resources Online?

Although transitioning your traditional, face-to-face course to a blended design can be a time-consuming process, there are several resources at your disposal. In this chapter, I describe some of these resources and offer suggestions for how to choose the materials that will best fit your course. Having clear goals and objectives (see Chapter 2) are the most important steps to choosing the materials and activities (both face-to-face and online) with which your students will engage to assist their learning.

Library Resources

Your campus library has a range of resources that may be helpful for your students' learning. Many library systems subscribe to databases that include scholarly articles, images, and videos. Often, these resources can be linked directly into your LMS course website for students to access directly. Additionally, many databases provide "permalinks" to share with students so that, as long as they are signed into the campus system, they can access the resources you provide quickly and easily.

Your library may have also created LibGuides, or sets of resources that are compiled by a librarian on particular topics (see Box 9.1). For example, there may be a LibGuide that explains the APA citation style or a LibGuide on how best to find primary sources in research. Many libraries also create specific LibGuides that can be used for courses or assignments so that students can get started with a set of materials.

Your library may also have access to additional subscriptions such as citation guides, streaming video collections, or other resources that can be easily embedded into your blended course. As you design your blended course, consider partnering with a librarian so that you can fully implement and utilize the resources available through your campus library.

Publisher Resources

More and more publishers are creating online materials that can be purchased along with a course textbook. Some examples of these materials might include flashcards, problem sets, case studies, videos, or other content that is digitally based (see Box 9.2). Although these resources are often offered at an additional cost to the student, they can be helpful supplements for students who prefer to learn with digital materials. Additionally, some of the publisher materials include homework sets that can be

BOX 9.1
What Is a LibGuide?

A LibGuide is a set of webpages that librarians create to help their patrons with research, learn more about a particular topic, or integrate into a particular course or assignment.

BOX 9.2
Accessibility Note

Although publisher resources can be an incredible addition to a blended course, it is important to check with your campus's disability services professionals to make sure that the online materials are accessible for all learners. For example, some adaptable learning technologies can be difficult for screen-readers to translate to learners who have visual impairments.

automatically graded, thus increasing instructor efficiency. Many publishers have sales representatives assigned to different campuses who can answer questions about the online materials associated with any textbook or disciplinary area. You can also contact your campus bookstore or academic technology unit to learn more about the kinds of online materials that other instructors may have already used on your campus.

Open Educational Resources

Another growing area of online materials being used in blended and fully online courses is open educational resources (OERs). OERs are "educational materials either licensed under an open copyright license or in the public domain" (Wiley, Bliss, & McEwan, 2014, p. 781). According to Atkins, Brown, and Hammond (2007), these materials can include "full courses, course materials, modules, textbooks, streaming videos, tests, software, and any other tools, materials, or techniques used to support access to knowledge" (p. 5). Often, OERs use a Creative Commons license to define how the materials can be used and shared. Creative Commons, founded in 2001, is a website that allows individuals or organizations to "dedicate their creative works to the public domain or retain their copyright while licensing them as free for certain uses, on certain conditions" (Atkins et al., 2007, p. 14). There are currently six different licenses that are denoted by symbols that can be added to a print work, website, or other creation (see Box 9.3).

Scholars such as Wiley, Bliss, and McEwan (2014) have noted five key challenges to working with OERs:

1. *They can be hard to find.* OERs can be a challenge to locate despite several "repositories" that have been created. Later in the chapter, I share a range of web resources to help you locate OERs of different types.

BOX 9.3
Creative Commons Attribution Licenses

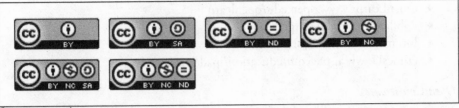

Source. www.creativecommons.org

2. *They lack sustainability.* Some OERs are grant-funded and need to be maintained upon creation. Other OERs are created by individuals and shared with the public, but may not be regularly updated. In simple terms, an OER that works for you this term may be hard to find or out-of-date six months from now.

3. *They can be too localized.* If an OER is created for a particular course or subject area, it may not be able to be used "as is" by others in different disciplines, campus locations, or countries.

4. *Their quality can be questionable.* Since there is no quality control for OERs, you will need to carefully check the materials to make sure they are accurate, easy to use, and complete. Some repositories for OERs have peer-review systems that allow users to rate OERs and share reviews to help you gauge the quality of materials.

5. *People who use OERs often do not "remix" them.* Although many OERs allow for changes to be made under the materials' licensing agreement, many people who use OERs prefer not to make changes and to use the materials as they are. Scholars have found that it is rare for people using OERs to revise or augment the materials before their use.

Another key concern for OERs is that, like the publisher materials mentioned previously, they may not be accessible for all learners. It is recommended that you check all OERs you plan to use in your blended course with your Office of Disability Services to ensure compliance with online accessibility standards.

Where to Find OERs

To help you locate OERs for potential use in your courses, you can start by checking out the following websites (as of this writing, the links included in this chapter are live; as stated previously the sustainability of OERs can be a challenge to finding free materials):

OER Repositories

These are web-based collections of OERs that are collected and searchable, often by category, type of OER, language, or age-group.

- Multimedia Educational Resource for Learning and Online Teaching (MERLOT): www.merlot.org/merlot/index.htm (read more about MERLOT in Malloy and Hanley, 2001)

- WikiEducator: http://wikieducator.org/Main_Page
- Internet Archive: https://archive.org
- OpenLearn: www.open.edu/openlearn
- ibiblio: www.ibiblio.org/about
- Jorum (UK): http://jorum.ac.uk
- iTunesU: ww.apple.com/education/ipad/itunes-u

Open Courseware

Smith and Casserly (2006) describe open courseware as including "lecture notes, reading lists, course assignments, syllabi, study materials, problems sets and exams, illustrations and simulations, and streaming videos of in-class lectures" (p. 11).

- Carnegie Mellon's Open Learning Initiative: https://oli.cmu.edu
- MIT Open Courseware: http://ocw.mit.edu/index.htm
- Open Education Consortium: www.oeconsortium.org
- Open Tapestry: http://ocwfinder.com
- Penn State's College of Earth and Mineral Sciences: http://open.ems.psu.edu

Information Resources/Community of Experts

These are searchable websites that collate a large body of information compiled by a range of experts.

- Wikipedia: www.wikipedia.org
- Decameron Web: www.brown.edu/Departments/Italian_Studies/dweb index.php
- Smarthistory: http://smarthistory.khanacademy.org

eBooks

- Project Gutenberg: www.gutenberg.org/wiki/Main_Page
- Wikibooks: http://en.wikibooks.org/wiki/WB:SUBJECT
- FullBooks: www.fullbooks.com
- Google Books: http://books.google.com
- Page by Page: www.pagebypagebooks.com/authorlist.html

Videos

- TED talks: www.ted.com
- Khan Academy: www.khanacademy.org
- YouTube: www.youtube.com (read more in Berk, 2009)
- Teach with Movies: www.teachwithmovies.org
- PBS Video: http://video.pbs.org

Images

- Flickr: www.flickr.com
- Everystockphoto: www.everystockphoto.com (use advanced search to Creative Commons–licensed)
- NIH Photo Galleries: www.nih.gov/about/nihphotos.htm

Sound

- The Freesound Project: www.freesound.org

Open Textbooks

- MERLOT Open Textbooks: www.merlot.org/merlot/materials.htm ?keywords=open+textbooks
- Texbookmedia: www.textbookmedia.com/Products/BookList.aspx
- Open Book Project: http://openbookproject.net

E-Journals

- Directory of Open Access Journals: www.doaj.org
- E-journals.org: www.e-journals.org
- Education-specific: http://aera-cr.asu.edu/ejournals

Government Publications

- Catalog of U.S. Government Publications: http://catalog.gpo.gov/F

A Step-by-Step Guide to Finding Resources Online

Online Resources Scavenger Hunt

Complete each of the following tasks to start a list of resources for your blended course. While working through the scavenger hunt, keep in mind that just because a resource looks like it would be fun for your students, it may not be aligned with your intended outcomes (see Chapter 5 for more on designing effective learning activities).

1. Find one online resource that you can plug in to your course with *no changes* that is directly applicable to your discipline (HINT: try looking for videos, modules, games, etc.).
2. Look through the MERLOT offerings and find one resource that you might *adapt* for your class.
3. Find a YouTube or TED Talk video that is applicable for your intended outcomes.

4. Find an online assessment tool that you might want to use in your course (HINT: try looking for quizzes, survey tools, learning style assessments or inventories, etc.).
5. Locate a diagram that explains a component of your course content.
6. Find a podcast (or episode of a podcast) applicable to your intended outcomes (HINT: you can start with the iTunes podcast store or "Podomatic" to find free episodes).
7. Find an appropriate article for your students to read in your library's online databases.
8. Find an appropriate blog post for your students to read that is applicable for your intended outcomes.

Assessing the Quality of Online Materials

Before beginning your search for online materials, I recommend answering the following guiding questions:

1. If I could imagine ideal supplemental materials to help my students learn this content, what would they look like?

2. What skills do I want my students to practice?

There are many different online resources that might be useful to you as you teach your blended courses. Take a look and explore more fully—noting the potential benefits and challenges—of different resources that might be useful for you (see Table 9.1).

Several assessment tools have been created to help instructors decide whether an online resource will work for their course. I recommend the following rubrics that cover a range of questions, including whether the online resource is accessible for all students:

- Learning Object Review Instrument (LORI) (Lealock & Nesbit, 2007): www.transplantedgoose.net/gradstudies/educ892/LORI1.5.pdf
- Achieve OER Rubric: www.achieve.org/files/AchieveOERRubrics.pdf

TABLE 9.1.
Potential Benefits and Challenges of Online Resources

Resource	Potential Benefits	Potential Challenges

TABLE 9.2.
Choosing Online Materials Checklist

	Yes	*No*	*Comments*
Does the online resource fit with my learning objectives for the week?	☐	☐	
Does the online resource promote active learning?	☐	☐	
Does the online resource help me to assess my students' learning?	☐	☐	
Is the online resource accessible for all students?	☐	☐	
Is the online resource easy for students to find and navigate?	☐	☐	
Does the online resource include clear instructions for students (if applicable)?	☐	☐	
Do I need to create any supplemental materials to help students learn through this online resource?	☐	☐	
Would this online resource work better if paired with another online resource?	☐	☐	
Is this the best online resource I can find to help my students learn this material?	☐	☐	

Finally, I offer a quick checklist (see Table 9.2) as you find resources that you might want to incorporate into your blended course.

Integrating Online Materials

Gurell (2008) recommends eight steps to integrating OERs into a course:

1. Assess the validity and reliability of the OER;
2. Determine placement within the curriculum, if not already done;
3. Check for license compatibility;
4. Eliminate extraneous content within the OER (assuming the license permits derivatives);
5. Identify areas of localization;
6. Remix with other educational materials, if applicable;
7. Determine the logistics of using the OER within the lesson;
8. Devise a method of evaluation or whether the currently planned evaluation needs adjustment. (p. 140)

Creating OERs

Several resources also exist if you are interested in creating your own online resources to share with the academic community:

- Tutorials by Open e-Learning Content Observatory Services (OLCOS): www
  .olcos.org/tutorials/as-pdf-documents/index.htm
- A unit on creating OERs by The Open University: www.open.edu/openlearn/
  education/creating-open-educational-resources/content-section-0

See more about creating multimedia resources in Chapter 10.

Key Ideas From Chapter 9

- There is a wide range of already existing materials that can be used to help
  students learn within your blended course.
- Instructors should think creatively about the kinds of learning materials and
  resources that could be used to help students learn.
- Some online learning materials and Open Educational Resource repositories
  are more sustainable than others.
- OERs are constantly being created, so instructors should always be on the
  lookout for additional materials that can enhance student learning in the
  blended environment.
- Not all of the materials available online are accessible for all students,
  particularly those who need to employ a screen-reader.

Questions for Faculty

- What resources does your library have that you can leverage for your blended
  course materials?
- Who is the person to talk with in your Office of Disability Services to ensure
  that the online materials you find for your course are accessible for all learners?
- Are there any publishers who have online materials that would work well for
  your blended course?

Questions for Administrators

- Does your institution have any e-policies regarding online materials or OERs
- Does your LMS have any active plug-ins with publishers that will ensure a
  student's ease of use with online materials?
- Is there a point-person identified within your Office of Disability Services
  to help instructors check online materials for compliance with accessibility
  standards?
- To what degree has your library system marketed e-learning materials in its
  collection so that instructors are aware of them?

Documenting Your Course Design Progress

TABLE 9.3.
Documenting Your Course Design Progress

Course Design Steps	*In Your LMS Sandbox*
• Explore the publisher resources available for your course to see if there are any that might be appropriate to include. • Complete the "Online Resources Scavenger Hunt" included in this chapter to find already-existing multimedia that relates to your course content. • Use Table 9.1 to develop a potential list of OERs that might be appropriate to include in your course. • Assess the list you created in Table 9.1 using the checklist in Table 9.2. • Schedule an appointment with your disability services office to ensure that any OERs that you choose for your course are accessible for all students.	• Explore the tools available in your LMS for creating "Learning Modules," a tool that can offer a helpful structure for organizing different pieces of course content including OERs. • If appropriate for your course, create a Learning Module on a topic of your choice using the tool in your LMS. • Using the list you created in Table 9.1 and that you assessed with Table 9.2, begin integrating OERs library material, or publisher materials that are most appropriate for your course into your LMS.

NOTES

10

CREATING MULTIMEDIA
RESOURCES

What Do We Know About Creating Multimedia Resources?

When creating your blended course, you may find yourself in need of multimedia resources that are specific to your course goals and learning objectives and not readily available online. A basic definition of *multimedia* is resources that combine both words and pictures (Mayer, 2005). Multimedia can be an effective resource for student learning because it presents information in multiple formats and can serve a variety of learning preferences simultaneously (Berk, 2009). For example, a short video demonstration with a voice-over lecture could benefit both visual and auditory learners. Additionally, there is evidence that the combination of words and graphics is particularly helpful to novice learners, or students who are new to a content area (Clark & Mayer, 2008, pp. 68–69). Borup, West, and Graham (2013) also found that asynchronous videos helped students to feel connected to their instructors and that the videos improved the social presence in the online environment (see Chapter 8 for more information about fostering social presence). Multimedia can also benefit students when they are asked to create it. Pegrum, Bartle, and Longnecker (2015) found that when students were asked to create their own podcasts related to course content, the students had better understanding and retention of the course materials. Multimedia such as video clips or interactive textbooks may also help make learning more engaging for students who are used to seeking out similar resources for entertainment purposes.

Mayer (2008) has articulated the following evidence-based principles of multimedia design: (a) reduce extraneous material; (b) highlight essential material; (c) do not add on-screen text to narrated animation; (d) place printed words next to corresponding graphics; (e) present corresponding narration and animation at the same time; (f) present animation in learner-paced segments; (g) provide pre-training in the name, location, and characteristics of key components; (h) present words as spoken text rather than printed text; (i) present words and pictures rather than words alone; and (j) present words in conversational style rather than formal style. These principles are meant to help instructors design materials that will be the most easily processed by learners. As you can see, Mayer recommends presenting simple multimedia resources, broken down into digestible pieces, where text and visuals are purposefully combined.

While you do not want to recreate the wheel with multimedia (see Chapter 9), if you do find yourself in a situation where you are producing your own resources there are some best practices to keep in mind. In this chapter, I provide suggestions and resources for the production of two kinds of multimedia resources: videos (visual recordings with audio) and podcasts (primarily audio recordings that can also include video). If you plan to produce either of these kinds of multimedia on your own, I recommend that you first contact the academic technology unit on your campus to see what kinds of training and support they can provide. The guidelines and suggestions in this chapter will offer a general introduction for creating multimedia resources, but your campus may have more specific instructions and support for particular software packages and tools.

A Step-by-Step Guide to Creating Multimedia Resources

General Principles for Creating Multimedia Resources

Before deciding which multimedia resources will be the right ones for your course, there are a few general principles to keep in mind:

Be as Evergreen as Possible

When creating multimedia, be careful not to make date-specific references (i.e., "this module will help prepare you for the exam next Monday") or to use examples that will not be timely the following term or in future course offerings (e.g., a news item that students will not remember, a popular culture reference that will quickly be dated). You want to create multimedia that you will be able to recycle in future courses so that you are not recreating lectures or tutorials every time you teach your blended course.

Make Sure the Multimedia You Create Is Accessible For All Learners

When creating any form of multimedia, it is important to keep in mind that your course may include students with sensory or other disabilities that might impact their use of the resources you create. For both videos and podcasts, the best practice is to create captions or a transcript that can be used by students who need them. If you have a disability services office on your campus, they may be able to help you with this or to provide additional resources or support.

Apply Principles of Cognitive Load to the Resources You Create

Cognitive load is the "load imposed on working memory by information being presented" (Paas & Sweller, 2005, p. 40). Depending on how information is presented, small or large amounts of our working memory may be required to process the information. For example, consider a webinar presentation where there is a video of the presenter, an image of PowerPoint slides as the presenter speaks, a chat window for participants to ask questions, and a place to take notes as you watch and listen to the presentation. This kind of environment can be taxing for your working memory because it is hard to know where to look and where your attention should be. There are several elements of the environment that are competing with one another for the audience members' attention. Try to create multimedia resources that utilize words and pictures effectively, but that are not overwhelming or confusing to students who are trying to learn the material being presented.

Best Practices for Creating Multimedia Resources

In additional to the general principles mentioned, when creating your video or podcast keep the following best practices in mind:

Know the Goal

What is the purpose of the multimedia resource? What do you want students to know or be able to understand once they have interacted with it? Make sure to start the video or podcast by stating the goal or intended outcomes so that students know the purpose of the resource.

Create an Outline

Write a short outline or script for yourself before you start the video or podcast so you have a sense of what you want to say and in what order. This can cut down on editing later.

Keep it Short

To harness your students' attention spans, try to keep your video or podcast to no longer than 10 minutes. This allows your students to watch it all in one sitting and be able to digest it in full. Also, short videos or podcasts are easier to rerecord if you make a mistake or need to change information in the video or podcast at a later date.

Use Active Learning Methods

Give your students something to think about while they are watching the video or listening to the podcast by asking questions during the video or podcast or giving students a short worksheet to fill out while interacting with the resource. These questions or worksheets can be posted alongside the video or podcast in your LMS.

Try for the Best Production Value Possible

A shaky camera or poor sound can hinder students' learning, so try to get the best recording atmosphere that you can. Check to see if there is equipment on your campus that can help with production value. Some campuses have a studio where these kinds of multimedia resources can be produced. At the very least, if you are recording yourself, pay attention to what is in the background of the video or podcast so that you do not accidentally include something in the shot or audio that you did not intend to (this is especially true when recording at home).

TABLE 10.1.
Multimedia Creation Template

Goal (state at the beginning of the multimedia resource):	
Outline (talking points to refer to when recording): • _____ • _____ • _____ • _____ • _____ • _____	
Active learning methods (accompanying worksheets or activities):	Supplemental resources (associated readings, websites, images, or other materials to contextualize the multimedia presentation):
Self-assessment activity (quiz, discussion board posting, problem-set, or other follow-up activity to gauge students' understanding of the multimedia resource):	

Provide Supplemental Resources

Have your students read a short article, visit a website, or look through some images before or after watching your video or listening to your podcast to help contextualize what they will be learning. Combining multimedia with other course resources can help students become more engaged in the course content.

Follow Up With a Self-Assessment

Consider asking your students to take a short quiz, post on a discussion board, or complete a problem set after they have watched your video or listened to your podcast to self-assess their understanding of the material. This can also help you to evaluate which videos or podcasts are most effective in helping your students learn.

Table 10.1 offers a Multimedia Creation Template using these criteria.

Tools for Creating Videos

There are several different kinds of videos that you might want to create for your blended course. Three common types of videos used in blended courses are:

BOX 10.1
Best Practice Tip

Some faculty who know they will be teaching a blended course far enough in advance might be tempted to record lectures from their face-to-face version of the same course to post online. This is not ideal. Because those lectures often include questions from the audience, have poor production quality in terms of visual and sound, and are quite lengthy, it is recommended that you break down your already existing lectures into smaller pieces and rerecord them for the blended course environment. Since you are redesigning the course for the blended modality, you may also find that other changes in the course structure necessitate revisions to your lectures.

1. *Lectures*: Videos in which you are directly talking to the camera and offering content delivery to your students or videos in which you are sharing a PowerPoint or other visual and offering voice-over content delivery. (See Box 10.1 for a best practice tip.)
2. *Tutorials*: Videos that are meant to teach students how something works. For example, you might record a tutorial for how to use a particular piece of software, or how to conduct a database search. Tutorials can be very detail oriented and may only be for a specific audience (e.g., students who are struggling with a particular concept).
3. *Demonstrations*: Videos that show students a step-by-step guide or process to follow in order to complete a task or use a particular tool. Often, they are more of a broad overview of a concept, idea, or theory. A common demonstration video might be to model for students how to effectively take notes while completing a course reading.

Depending on the kind of videos that you want to create, there is a range of software packages (some free and some not) that can help you to record videos for your course:

- Camtasia: www.techsmith.com/camtasia.html
- Panopto: www.panopto.com
- Tegrity: www.mhhe.com/tegrity
- Capture for Chrome: www.mediacore.com/screen-capture

These tools allow you to use a web camera (sometimes one is built into your computer) to record either yourself speaking, capture something that is happening on your screen, or both simultaneously. Sometimes these tools are called Lecture Capture or Screen Capture software. There are also different mobile device applications that can help you record video (see Chapter 11 for more information on mobile device software applications). Your institution may have invested in one software in particular, so check with your academic technology unit before purchasing something yourself. Your academic technology unit may also have a web camera that you can use if you do not already have one.

Tools for Creating Podcasts

Podcasts are a medium for content delivery that are simple to create and share. Since many podcasts do not include a visual element, it is easy for your students to listen to the content while on their commute to campus or while they are somewhere like the gym (although this might not be the ideal place to experience the content delivery). Podcasts are also easy to store and listen to from a mobile device. If you are new to podcasts, consider choosing some to listen to so that you can experience the different kinds of production involved with the range of shows that are available.

Since your students will be primarily listening to the content delivery with a podcast, consider supplementing the audio recording with one of the following:

- Questions to answer while listening
- Guided notes to complete while listening
- A set of questions to complete after listening to post to a discussion board for additional conversation with classmates
- A task to complete after listening to demonstrate their understanding

In addition to recording lectures for your students to listen to, podcasts are also an excellent medium for you to share interviews with different colleagues or experts in your field. Since you only need to record the audio for the podcast, these interviews can be conducted over the phone, or through a software tool like Skype or Google Hangout. Interviews or conversations about your course content can be a unique addition to your blended course that can broaden students' understanding of the course material and help to keep them engaged with the content delivery for the course.

To produce a podcast episode, you will need a good quality microphone and audio recording software (your academic technology unit may be able to help you with both of these if you do not already have them). Similar to the videos discussed previously, there are a range of software packages (some free and some not) that can help you to record podcasts for your course:

- Audacity: www.audacityteam.org
- Hipcast: www.hipcast.com

Also, many of the video recording and lecture capture software packages described in this chapter will allow you to create an audio file that can be turned into a podcast.

Post-Production

Many of the software packages mentioned previously include some form of editing software that you can use to revise the video and audio files that you create. Although you want to have good production quality for your multimedia, you should not worry about the videos or audio recordings being perfect—after all, you may stumble over your words in a real-life lecture that you would give face-to-face. When creating multimedia, do not let the perfect be the enemy of the good. Students will enjoy a certain level of you being human.

Once you have created your multimedia, you need to decide where to post it for students to access the resource. In addition to your LMS, there are free resources for posting videos (a common one is creating a YouTube channel) and for posting podcasts (a common one is iTunes; although keep in mind that with this option, you will need to host the media files yourself, but then you can include the podcast in the iTunes directory). Both YouTube and iTunes offer detailed instructions for how to use their services, but posting video and audio files to your LMS may be the most convenient place for students to find the content delivery medium that you choose.

Key Ideas From Chapter 10

- If you plan to produce your own multimedia, contact the academic technology unit on your campus to see what kinds of training and support they can provide.
- When creating multimedia resources for your blended course, you should try to make them evergreen and ensure they are accessible for all learners.
- You should be careful not to cognitively overload your students with the multimedia that you create.
- Multimedia resources should be created with a specific purpose and audience in mind.

Questions for Faculty

- What kinds of multimedia resources already exist for your course (see Chapter 9) and what do you need to create to supplement those resources?
- Thinking about the course goals and learning objectives for your course (see Chapter 2), what kinds of multimedia resources might be most helpful for your students' learning?
- What software packages and tools already exist on your campus that you can utilize to create multimedia resources?
- Does your campus offer trainings or tutorials for any software packages or tools that you plan to use to create the multimedia resources for your course?

Questions for Administrators

- Does your campus have particular software packages and tools that you would prefer faculty use when they create multimedia resources?
- How will you ensure that the multimedia resources created by faculty are accessible to all learners?
- What kinds of trainings or tutorials exist on your campus to help faculty create multimedia resources?

Documenting Your Course Design Progress

TABLE 10.2.
Documenting Your Course Design Progress

Course Design Steps	In Your LMS Sandbox
• Outline and record a short lecture video for your course using the template provided to see if video lectures might be a component you want to include in your course. • Check to see what campus resources are available to ensure the best production quality for your multimedia resources. • Ask around to see if colleagues in your department have created multimedia resources; what campus or online resources did they find to be the most helpful?	• Explore the different technologies available at your institution for video creation and lecture capture. • Choose a technology platform for creating videos in your blended course. • Create a lecture video and post within your LMS sandbox. • Create and post supplementary resources for video lectures or podcasts so that your students can actively engage with the multimedia resources (see Chapter 5 for more on designing effective learning activities).

NOTES

II

MOBILE DEVICES, APPS, AND SOCIAL MEDIA

With Victoria Wallace

What Do We Know About Mobile Devices, Apps, and Social Media?

Mobile devices and social media offer a range of tools to help you and your students meet the learning objectives of your course, but it is important not to overwhelm your students, or yourself, with too many tools at once. Since the blended environment is new for many students, making sure that you are intentionally incorporating technologies that are tied to the course goals and objectives is critical for your blended course design. We start with a review of some of the current research on the use of mobile devices and social media in the higher education classroom, paying particular attention the benefits and challenges associated with both. In this chapter, we also provide an overview of some of the more popular software applications for mobile devices, also known as apps, and social media platforms that may be of interest to blended instructors. Each app or platform is described alongside suggestions for how to use the component in a blended course. Although not all blended instructors will want to incorporate the use of mobile devices or social media platforms into their courses, at the end of the chapter we provide a step-by-step guide for how to choose the right app or social media platform if you choose to do so.

Mobile Devices and Apps

Increasing numbers of students are bringing technology with them into the classroom. A 2014 Pearson study found that although 89% of students are most likely to use laptops on a regular basis for their schoolwork, the numbers of students using smartphones and tablets continue to grow, with 83% of students regularly using a smartphone and 45% regularly using a tablet (Harris Poll, 2014). The 2015 Horizon Report (Johnson, Adams Becker, Estrada, & Freeman, 2015) notes that the bring-your-own-device (BYOD) phenomenon has become a significant development in higher education. BYOD allows for students to engage with personalized content since each student can set up their device to include apps and specifications of their choice. As Johnson and colleagues (2015) note, the BYOD movement can be helpful to learning because students' "devices are already populated with productivity apps . . . helping them to better organize their notes, syllabi, and schedules on campus and beyond" (p. 37). *Apps*, simply defined as mini software applications on mobile devices, are designed to complete a specific task or function. Much of the research that has been conducted on the use of apps in the classroom has focused on the integration of mobile devices such as tablets (Hofstein et al., 2013; Nguyen, Barton, & Nguyen, 2015; Peluso, 2012; Rossing, Miller, Cecil, & Stamper, 2012) and smartphones (Gikas & Grant, 2013).

To date, there is little empirical research regarding a relationship between mobile device use in the classroom and increases in student learning outcomes. While mobile devices have been found to increase the engagement of students (e.g., see Diemer, Fernandez, & Streepey, 2012; Shuler, Hutchins, & LaShell, 2010), other studies have found that the devices cause distractions for students when not used for learning purposes (e.g., see Gikas & Grant, 2013, p. 23; Rossing et al., 2012, p. 11; Wakefield & Smith, 2012). Overall, however, students have a positive perception about mobile learning in the classroom and are open to seeing expanded use of mobile devices for learning (Alrasheedi, Capretz, & Raza, 2015; Martin & Ertzberger, 2013). Both the challenges and benefits mentioned previously point to the need to intentionally and purposefully include mobile technologies in the blended classroom.

Because of their ready availability among students, mobile devices offer an opportunity to increase interactivity in the face-to-face component of the blended classroom. For example, services such as Poll Everywhere (www.polleverywhere .com) allow instructors to ask students questions, gather responses in real time, and share the responses with the group through the use of text messaging. Several student response systems (i.e., clickers) offer mobile apps rather than requiring students to purchase clicker hardware. LMSs like Blackboard Learn and Desire2Learn also offer apps for mobile phones and tablets. There are literally hundreds of apps that could be selected to enhance a learner's experience depending on your course content and learning objectives, and the list keeps growing every year. To better understand what is available, search Google for "apps in higher education" or use the search feature in app stores like iTunes. There are also apps developed to help you find apps: AppAdvice and AppShopper are two examples.

Mobile devices that have wireless Internet connection also allow students to conduct real-time research in the classroom because they have access to web browsers through their tablets or smartphones. Additionally, the uses of tablets, in particular, have been found to aid transition to a paperless classroom environment (Hofstein et al., 2013). When chosen and implemented thoughtfully, mobile devices and apps can foster student engagement and offer unique learning and assessment opportunities (Martin & Ertzberger, 2013). Later in the chapter we offer some examples of apps commonly found in the higher education classroom.

Social Media Platforms

Social media platforms are web-hosted spaces where people connect to share information and collaborate on ideas (Joosten, 2012). Some examples of the most popular social media platforms include Facebook, Twitter, Instagram, YouTube, and Pinterest. Blogging and wikis are also well-known social media activities, and these platforms are sometimes built right into an LMS. All social media allow for communication, collaboration, and sharing which make them ripe for classroom integration. The

2014 Horizon Report noted the "growing ubiquity of social media" as a "fast trend" (Johnson, Adams Becker, Estrada, & Freeman, 2014, p. 8) that will contribute to changes in higher education classrooms in the immediate future. As students (and their instructors) are using social media extensively in their personal lives, it is not surprising that this medium for social interaction online would also be implemented in the classroom. It is important to note, however, that most students use social media for social activities; they may not have considered the full extent to which social media can help with their learning (Clark et al., 2009; Wodzicki, Schwämmlein, & Moska-liuk, 2012).

Although Tess (2013) found that most existing research does not empirically support social media effectiveness in the classroom beyond self-reported data, some of the research is encouraging. For example, advocates for social media report greater student engagement and interest, improved communication, self-regulation, and self-efficacy (Blankenship, 2011; Guy, 2012). Additionally, social media has been found to inspire creativity, foster openness, and build valuable career skills (Blankenship, 2011; Guy, 2012). There is also some evidence that social media fosters relationships and, for students, can turn a list of unfamiliar peer names into a cohesive, collabo-rative community (Wolfman-Arent, 2014). Some research also points to improved learning; for example, in one study, wiki-related activities were found to help students achieve learning outcomes better than other social media and face-to-face activities, and students who were most active in the wiki obtained higher scores in the course (Laru, Näykki, & Järvelä, 2012).

While there are many advantages to social media in the classroom, it is not with-out controversy (Watts, 2014). Privacy and other ethical concerns have been found to be the primary challenges with social media use (Al-Bahrani & Patel, 2015; Barczyk & Duncan, 2013; Everson, Gundlach, & Miller, 2013; Graham, 2014). If not care-fully managed and if expectations are not explicitly stated, social media can quickly turn into an unpleasant experience and, at worst, a legal issue. Many institutions now have social media policies on their campus, so it is best to check to see what support and policies already exist on your campus. Current best practice suggests allowing students to voluntarily participate and providing explicit guidelines around what content should be shared within the course social media site. It is important to include a statement in your syllabus outlining these expectations (see Box 11.1 for an example).

Lastly, you will want to familiarize yourself with the social media platform's security settings and always test functionality and applicability before assigning any activities on social media to your students. It is best for you to experience first-hand any hurdles and challenges that your students may experience; this will also allow you to make adjustments to the assignment or activity as needed.

Social media can be used for a variety of purposes from instructional activities and self-reflection exercises to improving engagement and building community. Despite the concerns, many educators find the advantages to using social media in the class-room outweigh the challenges. One thing is clear: social media in the classroom is

BOX 11.1
Example of Facebook Intended Use and Policy Syllabus Statement

Although not specifically endorsed by coordinators and faculty of the department, a Facebook course site has been developed for the primary purpose of providing a forum for students to collaborate with each other, sharing course related information, study tips, and so on.

- Joining the Facebook page is completely voluntary
- To join, on Facebook, locate the "Course Name FB Page" and click on "Like" which will enable you to see posts and discussion in your news feed
- When posting links, please limit them to those pertaining to course content or other topics related to this course of study
- When making posts and commenting, please use common sense and professional language considering that Facebook is a public social network
- All posts must pertain to the course; please share non-course-related items on your personal Facebook pages.

Please note that faculty may or may not choose to monitor or participate in the Facebook page discussions.

Reproduced with permission from Margarita DiVall.

still in its infancy. The benefits and challenges must be carefully weighed, and should you choose to integrate social media into your teaching, intentionality and careful management are crucial. Later in the chapter, we offer examples of popular social media platforms used in higher education classrooms.

A Step-by-Step Guide to Mobile Devices, Apps, and Social Media

When choosing which apps or social media platforms to integrate into your course, ask yourself, what apps and social media platforms are you most comfortable with? What do you already know how to use? What apps and social media components are already available through your LMS? Then, you will want to consider what apps or social media platforms can be most supportive of your course goals and learning objectives. Table 11.1 offers a general checklist to consider when choosing an app or social media platform. Following the checklist are several common apps and social media platforms that can be utilized in higher education settings. We have also offered some suggestions for how you might use each app or social media platform to enhance your students' learning in your blended course and left space for you to write notes about your own ideas. Use the checklist in Table 11.1 as you explore the examples in this chapter, as well as when you look for additional examples on your own.

TABLE 11.1.
Choosing Apps and Social Media Checklist

	Yes	*No*	*Comments*
Does the app or social media platform fit with my learning objectives for the course?	☐	☐	
Does the app or social media platform promote active learning?	☐	☐	
Does the app or social media platform help me to assess my students' learning?	☐	☐	
Is the app or social media platform accessible for all students?	☐	☐	
Is the app or social media platform easy for students to find and navigate?	☐	☐	
Does the app or social media platform include clear instructions for students?	☐	☐	
Do I need to create any supplemental materials to help students learn through this app or social media platform?	☐	☐	
Would this app or social media platform work better if paired with another online resource?	☐	☐	
Is this the best app or social media platform I can find to help my students learn this material?	☐	☐	

Examples of Apps

Corkulous

Corkulous (www.corkulous.com) is a productivity app that allows users to collect ideas, create to-do lists, or set goals on a digital cork board. User-created cork boards can be shared with others to encourage communication and collaboration.

Ideas for Using Corkulous in the Blended Classroom

- Model productivity for your students by creating to-do lists in Corkulous.
- Have students use Corkulous to collect ideas for a group project or paper.
- Ask students to collaboratively set goals for what they want to accomplish during the semester using Corkulous. Check in on the goals at midterm to see what progress has been made.

- _____
- _____

Explain Everything

Explain Everything (www.explaineverything.com) is a digital whiteboard app that allows users to create and share videos. Videos could include working out problem sets, demonstrating how to use a website, annotating an article with notes, or other forms of tutorials. Voice recording is also available alongside the video recording, so students can hear an instructor's explanation as they watch the visual.

Ideas for Using Explain Everything in the Blended Classroom

- Create a video tutorial that walks students through navigating your course website or any specific tools that students will be using throughout the course such as discussion boards, chat features, blogs, or wikis.
- Video record a student performing a task. Provide annotation and voiceover in the video to highlight areas where the student needs improvement or correction.
- Ask each student to create a demonstration or explanation of a piece of the course content to share with their peers as a study aid.
- Offer extra demonstrations of problem sets or homework problems online by writing out the process for solving each problem and talking students through each solution.

- _____

- _____

Evernote

Evernote (www.evernote.com) is a comprehensive note-taking app that allows users to create lists, share ideas across devices, or otherwise manage projects. Users can handwrite notes within the app, take pictures of ideas or inspirations, and share what they have compiled with others.

Ideas for Using Evernote in the Blended Classroom

- Have students take notes on online content for the course in Evernote.
- Ask students to use Evernote to plan for papers and projects within the course, sharing their ideas and notes with you at predetermined times throughout the term.
- Share your own note-taking strategies with students through Evernote to model best practices.

- _____

- _____

Mindjet

Mindjet (www.mindjet.com) is a software app to help with mind mapping (also called "concept mapping"; see more in Chapter 4), a form of brainstorming where users can connect ideas visually to show relationships. Topics or ideas (including both text and images) within the mind map can be easily reorganized by "dragging and dropping" them to new locations.

Ideas for Using Mindjet in the Blended Classroom

- Develop mind maps using Mindjet to share an organizational structure for your course topics with students.
- Have students use Mindjet to create a mind map of the course for a final project.
- Ask students to use Mindjet to organize the course content into a study guide for upcoming exams.
- Have students brainstorm and create mind maps to plan projects and assignments to improve visual literacy.
- Select course topics or ideas students typically have a difficult time integrating and have students create a mind map explaining the relationships and connections between them.
- _____
- _____

ShowMe

ShowMe (www.showme.com) is a software application similar to Explain Everything that acts like a digital whiteboard. Users can easily create, record, and share tutorials (extensive examples are included on the ShowMe website).

Ideas for Using ShowMe in the Blended Classroom

- Create a video tutorial that walks students through navigating your course website or any specific tools that students will be using throughout the course such as discussion boards, chat features, blogs, or wikis.
- Ask each student to create a demonstration or explanation of a piece of the course content to share with their peers as a study aid.
- Ask students to find a tutorial relevant to your course on ShowMe's website and post a link to share with you and their peers.
- Offer extra demonstrations of problem sets or homework problems online by writing out the process for each problem and talking students through each solution.
- Illustrate calculations, diagrams, and solutions during lectures.
- _____
- _____

Examples of Social Media Platforms

Blogs

A blog (www.blogger.com or www.wordpress.com) is a "web log" where authors can "post" ideas or content on a particular topic. Some blogs have multiple authors who contribute posts. Most blog posts are organized reverse-chronologically, with the most recent post first. Blogs can be professional in tone or they can be more personal "web diaries" for the authors. Most blogs include a "comment" feature where readers can respond to an author's post with their own reactions, ideas, or feedback. Bloggers can include images, links, and videos along with the text in their posts. A more recent form of blogging that uses video as a primary platform is called "vlogging." Free blog platforms include Blogger, Tumbler, and Wordpress.

Ideas for Using Blogs in the Blended Classroom

- Ask students to keep a blog where they share their responses and analysis of course readings.
- Have students use blogs as a form of peer feedback where they read and respond to the work of their classmates.
- Ask students to find blogs of professionals in your discipline so that they can follow the most recent ideas related to the course content.

- _____

- _____

Twitter

Twitter (www.twitter.com) is a free social media platform where users can engage in a form of "micro-blogging" by posting "tweets" of 140 characters or less. Twitter users can "follow" other users and develop their own network of followers. Frequently, tweets are accompanied by a "hashtag" so that users can easily search for content. For example, on election night, tweets might include a hashtag of #democrat or #republican. When users click on a hashtag, they are shown all of the tweets using that tag, without having to follow all the users posting those tagged messages. Tweets can also include images and links. Many Twitter users use the platform to share news and commentary on popular culture.

Ideas for Using Twitter in the Blended Classroom

- Create a hashtag for comments related to your course to help build community online. You can post upcoming deadlines or resources for the course for students, and your students will have an extra way of contacting you and each other.
- Ask students to follow the tweets of particular users or a particular hashtag related to your course content.
- Have students practice writing concise thesis statements by posting their arguments in 140 characters or less.

- _____

- _____

Facebook

Facebook (www.facebook.com) is a free social media platform where users create a profile page and share education, family, and work information as well as their favorite books, television shows, and music. Users "friend" one another to build their network and can join group pages (private spaces set up for particular organizations to network with other Facebook users). Users post text, photo, or video "status updates" to share with their friends. A user's "timeline" will show a history of all the statuses posted by a user while the "newsfeed" shows a history of all the statuses posted by a user's Facebook friends.

Ideas for Using Facebook in the Blended Classroom

- Create a group page for your course. Have students post course-related questions, news events, and resources to share and help build community online. You can post upcoming deadlines or relevant articles for students to follow. Your students will also have an extra way of contacting you and each other.
- In your group page, poll your class using the poll app in Facebook.
- Have students follow politicians or prominent figures in your field of study who also have Facebook pages.
- Set up an avatar Facebook profile page. In your course group page, post content-related questions from your avatar Facebook account and ask students to respond. For example, a Maternity and Postpartum Healthcare course could include an avatar of a pregnant patient posing questions to the students related to her condition and various ailments.
- Have students in small working groups or study groups create their own group pages (and invite you so you can respond to questions and track students' progress).
- _____
- _____

LinkedIn

LinkedIn (www.linkedin.com) is a free social media platform where users can create a comprehensive professional "profile" that is similar to an online résumé. Users can "connect" with other users to build a professional network, receive or give recommendations based on previous professional experiences, join groups (e.g., a college or university alumni group), and look for jobs. LinkedIn provides recommendations and prompts for the kinds of information that users might want to include, such as a picture of themselves, additional information about their previous jobs, publications, and other components that help to describe the user's professional life.

Ideas for Using LinkedIn in the Blended Classroom

- Ask students to find profiles of users that demonstrate the kinds of jobs they might pursue in your discipline.

- Have students critique an online profile that they think is not effective to demonstrate their awareness of online professionalism.
- Develop an assignment around students creating a comprehensive LinkedIn profile.
- Ask students to connect to one another on LinkedIn to help build their professional networks.

- _____

- _____

Pinterest

Pinterest (www.pinterest.com) is a free social media platform where users can create "boards" of images with short commentaries. Users can follow other users' boards or "re-pin" an image that another user has "pinned" to one of their boards. Pinterest offers users the opportunity to curate collections of images into their own organizational structures. Images that are pinned are frequently linked to the original source for the image.

Ideas for Using Pinterest in the Blended Classroom

- Ask students to introduce themselves to each other by creating boards on Pinterest that represent their identities and interests.
- Have students use Pinterest to collect ideas and sources for an upcoming paper, assignment, presentation, or large project.
- Create a visual glossary of terms for the course.
- Ask students to curate books, films, images, or other elements that are related to your course content.

- _____

- _____

Instagram

Instagram (www.instagram.com) is a free social media platform where users can share images accompanied by short commentary with other users. Frequently, images are accompanied by a hashtag so that users can easily search for content. For example, images of food might include a hashtag of #breakfast or #lunch. When users click on a hashtag, they are shown all of the images using that tag, without having to follow all the users posting those tagged messages. Instagram is used by many businesses to market products and has a wide base of individual users sharing personal and professional images with their followers.

How to Use Instagram in the Blended Classroom

- Have students create Instagram accounts to document their learning that is occurring outside of the classroom.

- Ask students to find Instagram users related to your course content (scientists, artists, musicians, writers, etc.) and to analyze the ways these professionals represent their work online.
- Create a class Instagram account and post images of students working together in the classroom when they are together face-to-face.
- _____
- _____

Key Ideas From Chapter 11

- There are a range of free and low-cost apps and social media platforms that can be used to engage students in learning.
- Apps and social media platforms should be chosen with care to ensure they are helping students meet the learning outcomes for the course.
- There may be similar features of different apps and social media already located within your LMS; consider making the most of these features rather than asking students to interact with more than one platform or pay for what they could get for free through the LMS (see Chapter 7 for more about common LMS features).
- A little goes a long way when it comes to apps and social media. Consider only implementing one new app or social media platform per course to keep from overwhelming students (and yourself).

Questions for Faculty

- What kinds of apps will improve or enhance the workflow of your blended teaching?
- Does your institution have a policy about how faculty members use apps or social media for traditional, blended, or online courses?
- Are regular trainings offered on apps and social media features?
- Does your institution have an Office of Disability Services and have they checked your apps or social media platform to see if they are accessible for all learners, particularly those with sensory disabilities?

Questions for Administrators

- Does your institution have a policy about how faculty members use apps or social media for traditional, blended, or online courses?
- Who supports apps and social media use at your institution? Does that person or office gather feedback from faculty and students about their use of apps and social media?

- Does your institution have an Office of Disability Services and have you created an institutional policy to have this office review blended courses before they are launched to ensure they are accessible for all learners, particularly those with sensory disabilities?
- Do you have an institutional structure through which you can discuss technology tool integration, e-policies, and the evaluation of blended courses with department heads, IT professionals, and other institutional stakeholders?

Documenting Your Course Design Progress

TABLE 11.2.
Documenting Your Course Design Progress

Course Design Steps	In Your LMS Sandbox
<ul><li>Identify learning objectives where mobile devices or social media could enhance the learner experience.</li><li>Using Table 11.1, decide if you will be using any apps or social media in your blended course.</li><li>If you will be using apps or social media in your course, add descriptions or instructions about these components to your course syllabus.</li></ul>	<ul><li>If you will be using apps or social media in your course, add links to these components to your LMS sandbox.</li><li>Consider making a tutorial video for the app or social media platform that you choose to integrate into your course and adding this tutorial to your LMS sandbox.</li></ul>

NOTES

THE BLENDED COURSE
SYLLABUS

What Do We Know About the Blended Course Syllabus?

For a course being developed using backward design principles, the creation of the syllabus usually occurs toward the end of the design process. This is done to ensure the prioritization of fundamental design elements such as the intended outcomes, the assessments, and the learning activities for the course. Many of the activities you have completed thus far throughout the workbook will be useful to you as you begin to draft the syllabus for your blended course. As you will read in this chapter, there are several ways that a syllabus can be modified to acculturate students to a blended modality and to ensure their success. There are also two examples of blended course syllabi included in the appendices so that you can see how all of the syllabus elements work together.

Syllabi are seen by many as the cornerstone of a course, perhaps because a syllabus can serve many purposes (Fink, 2012). Research on syllabi design and the influence of syllabi design on student learning is broad. Scholars have studied the range of syllabi components (Eberly, Newton & Wiggins, 2001), how syllabi differ across disciplines (Albers, 2003), how students perceive syllabi (Calhoon & Becker, 2008; Harnish & Bridges, 2011; Saville, Zinn, Brown, & Marchuk, 2010), and how students use syllabi throughout a term (Becker & Calhoon, 1999), among other areas. There is even a scholarly journal called *Syllabus* that is devoted to explorations on the topic.

In the following section, I describe the purposes of syllabi that are included in the literature: (a) as contract or legal document, (b) as a permanent record, (c) as a resource for student learning, (d) as a motivational tool, (e) as an interaction tool, (f) as a collaboration tool, (g) as a socialization tool, (h) as a communication tool, (i) as an interpersonal tool, (j) as an administrative tool, (k) as a course or curriculum development tool, (l) as a professional development tool, and (m) as a marketing tool. Scholarly references regarding each of these syllabi purposes can be found in Appendix A.

Syllabus Purposes

As a Contract or Legal Document

Bers, Davis, and Taylor (1996) point to the administrative purposes of syllabi as public descriptions of courses, evidence in grievance debates, and documents used to provide evidence of course equivalency for credit transfer; several scholars argue that these purposes constitute the syllabus as a contract.

As a Permanent Record
Syllabi are permanent records for an individual's teaching career as well as for departmental or institutional curricular records.

As a Resource For Student Learning
The syllabus helps students to see what the instructor has prioritized for the course content and may also include information about instructional techniques and assessment that assist a student in succeeding in the course.

As a Motivational Tool
Estes (2007) argues that the syllabus should be seen "as a crucial document for conveying an approach and a mindset" (p. 184) for a particular course. The syllabus can help students to be excited about a course and to feel personal ownership over their learning.

As an Interaction Tool
For syllabi that have multimedia components, instructors can use the document to help students interact with one another and course materials from the beginning of a course.

As a Collaboration Tool
Some instructors ask students to collaboratively generate course rules, assignments, or readings that are then included in the syllabus.

As a Socialization Tool
Scholars have discussed how the syllabus is a tool to acculturate students into a higher education environment, a particular discipline, or a standard of behavior.

As a Communication Tool
Altman and Cashin (1992) argue that "the primary purpose of a syllabus is to communicate to one's students what the course is about, why the course is taught, and what will be required of the students for them to complete the course with a passing grade" (p. 1). Eberly, Newton, and Wiggins (2001) agree that "the syllabus is often the initial communication tool that students receive as well as being the most formal mechanism for sharing information with students regarding any course" (p. 56).

As an Interpersonal Tool
Several scholars have pointed to the ways in which tone and choice of language can impact students' perceptions of a course and a teacher.

As an Administrative Tool
Syllabi are used for the purposes of accreditation, evaluation of teacher effectiveness, and development of benchmarks for pedagogical initiatives such as learner-centeredness.

As a Course or Curriculum Development Tool

When looking to change or norm a department curriculum, syllabus analysis can be an important factor. The syllabus creates a record of how a course may change over time, acts as an artifact to pass along to colleagues new to teaching a course, and can help with multisection norming in larger courses.

As a Professional Development Tool

The literature shows disciplinary differences in syllabus components, so a discussion with department colleagues, or across disciplines, can result in interesting pedagogical conversation. Syllabi are also frequently used as job market materials. Lastly, syllabi can be used for publications in the *Scholarship of Teaching and Learning*.

As a Marketing Tool

The syllabus can be used as a tool to advertise a course, particularly in institutional settings where students are "shopping" for certain learning experiences.

Collins (1997) states that "the syllabus lets us help students think of themselves as insiders in the strange world built by academics, and the process of its construction and revision affords us periodically recurring opportunities to be self-critical about our course, its content, and our approach to it" (pp. 80–81). Indeed, the syllabus is a tool for reflection on our course design, pedagogical choices, and our goals for student learning. In the step-by-step guide that follows, you will be able to choose the various components to include in your syllabus and see a range of examples of statements that have been designed for blended course syllabi. As you explore the steps outlined in the remainder of the chapter for creating your course syllabus, I encourage you to reflect on the purposes your syllabus has served for your traditional courses and how a blended course syllabus may serve additional or different purposes.

A Step-by-Step Guide to the Blended Course Syllabus

Choosing Components of Your Blended Syllabus

Scholars who have studied syllabus components typically agree on the kinds of information that should be included. Scholarly references for each content area described in this section can be found in Appendix B.

Instructor Information

Includes instructor name, phone number, office location, office hours, and other pertinent contact information.

Course Information

Includes course title, location, time and days of meetings, and other logistical information about the course.

Course Description
Includes the course description offered in a curricular catalogue in addition to a description written by the instructor.

Course Rationale
Includes information about where the course fits within a curriculum, major, or minor field of study and why the course adds value to a student's education.

Pedagogical Methods or Instructional Techniques
Includes information about the instructor's choices regarding the structure of the course; the assignments, activities, or assessments used; and/or the classroom techniques (lecture, team-based learning) that the students will experience.

Readings/Materials and Textbooks
Includes information about the textbook, readings, course tools (calculators, etc.), and other materials and where these items can be found by the student (see Box 12.1).

Goals and Objectives
Includes information about what students will know, understand, and be able to do upon successfully completing a course (see Chapter 2 for additional information).

Calendar/Course Schedule
Includes information about when the course will meet, when readings and assignments are due, and when the course will not meet due to holidays.

Course Policies
Includes information about policies on attendance and participation, academic dishonesty, class behavior expectations, and other policies that apply to students taking the course.

Assignments
Includes information about the tasks, including tests and exams, that students will complete to earn their grade in the course.

Grading Procedures
Includes information about the course grading scale, the weights of different assignments and activities, and may also include rubrics or other assessment tools.

Support Services or Student Resources
Includes information about campus resources on disability services, student tutoring or writing center services, the campus wellness center, and other areas of support designed to help students succeed in their learning.

When considering the components for a blended course syllabus, I recommend the following:

Instructor Information

Make sure to differentiate between face-to-face and online office hours if you plan to offer one or both for your blended course. Checking in with students to make sure they know how to access online office hours is also a good idea.

Course Information

If the course is being taught in a blended modality for the first time, this may be something to include in the course information to encourage student feedback about the structure as well as to ask for their patience as you work out any issues that may arise with technology. (See Box 12.2 for an example syllabus statement.)

Course Description

Consider including a description or definition of the *blended learning model* along with the regular course description. This can be especially helpful for students who are experiencing blended learning for the first time.

Course Rationale

This is a space where you can offer a brief explanation of why the course was transitioned to a blended model. If you choose not to include this in your syllabus, you may want to discuss the rationale with students in the first class.

Pedagogical Methods or Instructional Techniques

If there are particular technologies or tools that will be integral to successful learning, you may want to include brief descriptions here along with your methods and techniques. This is another area of the syllabus where a definition of *blended learning* could also be included if not appended to the course description.

BOX 12.1
Example of Readings and Materials List

Required Textbook: *Business Statistics—Communicating with Numbers*, by Sanjiv Jaggia and Alison Kelly, 2013, McGraw-Hill Publishers, **WITH** McGraw-Hill's CONNECT (online assignment and assessment system). Choose <u>one</u> of the following options:

   a. eBook with CONNECT: Purchase CONNECT Plus from [LINK]
   b. New textbook packaged with CONNECT. Available at bookstore. After purchase, go to [LINK] and enter access code for CONNECT found on textbook.
   c. Used textbook and CONNECT purchased separately. Purchase CONNECT from [LINK]

Unless you are given a used text, the eBook with CONNECT is the most economical way to purchase the class materials. No matter which option you choose, after a one-time log in for CONNECT, you will be able to access all online components for the class directly from Blackboard.

Reproduced with permission from Alison Kelly.

BOX 12.2
Example of Blended Format Syllabus Statement

This course follows a *blended format* where the majority of the lectures are covered outside of class time. Class time is used to review the more difficult concepts and solve homework exercises and case studies. In-class and out-of-class requirements are as follows:

- In-class requirements: A weekly, 1.5-hour in-class meeting where we review the weekly assigned material and solve homework exercises and case studies. Students also take quizzes and exams during this time period (1.5 hours a week).
- Out-of-class requirements: Outside of class, students are required to complete assigned readings, watch video lectures, [and] complete conceptual exercises (referred to as LearnSmart) and online homework assignments. (10.5 hours a week).

Reproduced with permission from Alison Kelly.

BOX 12.3
Example of Statement Regarding Timeline for Blended Course Assignments

---

Prior to each in-class meeting, you are expected to:

- Complete all relevant readings,
- View online lectures (see Blackboard > Course Documents > Video folder), and
- Complete LearnSmart assignments (see Blackboard > Course Documents > CONNECT: LearnSmart folder).

Within 48 hours of each in-class meeting, you are expected to:

- Complete on-line homework assignment (see Blackboard > Course Documents > CONNECT: Homework Assignments folder).

Reproduced with permission from Alison Kelly.

Readings/Materials and Textbooks
If the course requires the use of a technology-enhanced textbook or other web-based tools, this is the place to explain where and how to access those tools. (See Box 12.2 for an example.)

Goals and Objectives
Make sure to include goals and objectives that are related to the use of technology or the blended environment if appropriate to your course. (You can read more about this in Chapter 2.)

Calendar/Course Schedule
I want to highlight the increased importance of the course schedule within a blended course syllabus. Students may initially be confused about the course structure, including

BOX 12.4
Example of Grade Book Statement

All grades will be available via the Grade Center on Blackboard. Please consider the online grade book as a courtesy to you, subject to errors given various upgrades and shifts in the software. I reserve the right to make grade book corrections to keep it consistent with the syllabus so that your grade reflects true performance, not software or user error. If you see something that doesn't make sense, please alert me! Thanks much for your help.

Reproduced with permission from Alison Kelly.

when they are supposed to attend face-to-face meetings or synchronous online sessions. Discussing the structure in person on the first day of class is highly recommended. (Examples of course schedules are provided in Chapter 6 on course mapping; see also Box 12.3)

Course Policies
If there are course policies that are specific to the blended learning experience (e.g., an online etiquette policy), make sure to include these as well.

Assignments
Because students may be experiencing blended learning for the first time, it is important to take special care to note whether assignments are due in class or online. Indicating how tests or exams will be administered will also be a crucial component of student success and comfort for the course (see Chapter 4 for more information about online assessment tools).

Grading Procedures
If you plan to share grades via your LMS, consider including a statement for students to share that information (e.g., see Box 12.4).

Support Services or Student Resources
If your institution has special support resources for blended courses, include them here.
   Two additional components are also helpful for blended courses: technology requirements and technology support services.

Technology Requirements
This area will include the kinds of technology tools (software and hardware) that a student will need to be successful in the course. Additionally, this may include a statement regarding required Internet speed.

Technology Support Services
This area will include contact information about campus support services for technology assistance for things such as set-up of technology, troubleshooting of technology, and support for a campus LMS. You may also choose to include embedded links

to tutorials or instructions for common technology issues or training associated with the course.

Lastly, when possible, it is recommended that you include hyperlinks within your syllabus to course resources, assignments, or other components that are available online. Students are more likely to actually review the materials you are pointing them toward if they have the direct means to access it.

Sharing Your Syllabus

Traditional, blended, and online courses frequently rely on an LMS to share information with students (for more information on LMSs, see Chapter 7). I recommend not only posting your blended course syllabus online for students to review before the course begins but also going over the syllabus during the first face-to-face class so that students can ask questions. Posting a discussion board thread (discussed more in Chapter 8) for student questions about the syllabus can also be a helpful method of sharing information with the whole group when one student asks a question that may be pertinent to everyone.

Although many instructors are used to discussing their syllabus within the first week of class only, Becker and Calhoon (1999) argue that "given the general trend for students, particularly continuing students, to pay less attention to syllabus items as the semester wears on, it would be wise to revisit portions of the syllabus in class with the students throughout the semester" (p. 10). I also recommend using the syllabus as a classroom resource that is referred to and reviewed frequently. By having the syllabus available online, students will be able to reference the document to find information about office hours and instructor contact information as well as to review course policies when needed.

Key Ideas From Chapter 12

- In the backward design process, the syllabus is typically drafted after more fundamental course design activities are completed.
- A syllabus can serve many purposes for students, faculty members, and administrators.
- A syllabus document can provide important information for students who are taking a blended course for the first time.
- The blended course syllabus has additional components (e.g., technology requirements and technology support services) that may not have appeared previously on an instructor's traditional course syllabus.

Questions for Faculty

- Does your institution or department have a syllabus template for traditional, blended, or online courses?

- Is there a model that you can use when designing your blended course syllabus from another faculty member who has successfully taught a blended course?
- What purposes has your syllabi served for your traditional courses? How might those purposes change for your blended course?

Questions for Administrators

- Does your institution have a syllabus template for traditional, blended, or online courses?
- Have you established mandatory, suggested, and optional syllabus components for blended courses?
- Does your institution have a repository (online or otherwise) for syllabi to be shared between faculty members?

Documenting Your Course Design Progress

TABLE 12.1.
Documenting Your Course Design Progress

Course Design Steps	In Your LMS Sandbox
<ul><li>Choose the components that you will include in your blended course syllabus and make a note of any modifications that might need to be made because of the blended modality.</li><li>Check to see if your campus has a syllabus template that is recommended for traditional, blended, or online courses.</li><li>Ask around to see if there are other instructors of blended courses who might be willing to share an example of their syllabus with you.</li><li>Begin drafting your blended course syllabus, adding in components that you have already designed from previous workbook activities.</li><li>Gather campus-specific resources and support structures to include in your syllabus (e.g., the help desk number for LMS-related questions).</li></ul>	<ul><li>Create a space for your course syllabus in your LMS sandbox navigation menu.</li><li>Upload your completed syllabus to your LMS site.</li><li>If you plan to have students complete a syllabus quiz, design the quiz in your LMS and place a link to the quiz in the same content area that you post the syllabus.</li></ul>

NOTES

13

PREPARING YOUR STUDENTS
FOR SUCCESS

What Do We Know About Preparing Your Students for Success?

As you may have gathered from the previous chapters, a lot goes into making your blended course an environment that is designed for student success. As Picciano (2009) argues, blended "instruction is not always just about learning content or a skill but is also about supporting students socially and emotionally" (p. 14). From the design of your LMS (see Chapter 7) to the inclusion of social presence elements throughout your online environment (see Chapter 8), all areas of your blended course should be created with student success in mind. This chapter will provide an overview of some additional components that you can add to your course to help students adjust to the blended course environment and to help them engage in metacognition, or the process of intentionally reflecting on their own learning, when using technology tools and resources.

De George-Walker & Keefe (2010) argue that key components of blended learning include instructors "supporting students in understanding what it is they are expected to learn, the choices they have available to them when learning and . . . assist[ing] them to develop the necessary skills of reflection, self-direction and self-management" (p. 3) needed to succeed in an autonomous learning environment. It is important for all students, but particularly for students who may not be as familiar with independent learning, to be properly acculturated to blended learning in the first weeks of the course to ensure their success navigating both the course structure and the course materials throughout the term.

According to Abel (2005), some of the most important supports for student success in online learning environments include: a "highly available website or course management system, [a] student phone help desk, [and an] orientation to online courses for students" (p. 2). While faculty teaching blended courses may not have control over all of these components, knowing where to send students when they need technical support, creating a robust online LMS site, and developing materials to help acculturate students to the blended environment are all things that instructors can do to prepare themselves to support students' success. (See Chapter 12 for more information about what to include in your blended course syllabus to support students.)

A Step-by-Step Guide to Preparing Your Students for Success

As you finalize the preparations for your course, take some time to think about what your students will know about blended learning. Are there resources on your campus, such as an online readiness quiz, that students can take to familiarize themselves with the differences between the traditional classroom and online learning components (see more regarding online readiness instruments in Dray et al., 2011; Hung, Chou, Chen, & Own, 2010; and Pillay, Irving, & Tones, 2007)? Is blended learning widespread enough on your campus that students will have heard about the classroom environment from their peers? Are there certain misconceptions that your students may bring to the classroom? (As an example, a common misconception is that blended learning is easier than a traditional classroom setting because students spend less time face-to-face with an instructor, but the opposite is often true because of the increase in independent learning and motivation required by the blended environment.) In the next activity, I offer several different questions for you to consider as you think about how best to acculturate your students to the blended environment. By answering these questions, you may be alerted to new areas where your students will need additional support and guidance. If you are not sure of the answer to one of the questions, use the space to brainstorm where you might find out the information.

What Do Students Know About Blended Learning?

1. What can I assume my students know about blended learning terminology?

2. What can I assume my students know about the technology tools and platforms used in my course?

3. What can I assume my students know about time management?

4. What can I assume my students know about communicating in online environments?

5. What can I assume my students know about how to use face-to-face class time?

Welcome Announcement and Email

Contacting your students electronically via email before your class begins is an excellent way to start acculturating them to the blended course environment (see

---

BOX 13.1
Example of Welcome Email and LMS Announcement

Email: Welcome to STATS250. Our first meeting is next Tuesday, January 15th at 10:00 a.m. in Archer 349. Before our first meeting, I have two tasks for you to complete. These tasks can be found on the Announcement page on the course's Blackboard site. (For those who are not familiar with Blackboard, visit the My Suffolk/Blackboard site, log in, choose Blackboard from the menu, and click on our class: 13SP-STATS-250-HYB1-Applied Statistics.)

Announcement: Prior to our first meeting on Tuesday, January 15th, I would like you to complete the following two tasks.

1. *Task 1: Get the syllabus*:
   - Print a copy of the syllabus. It is located under **Course Content** on **Blackboard**.
   - Read the syllabus. (You may purchase class materials before class, or you can wait until after our first meeting.)
   - On the first day of class, introduce yourself to me and let me initial your syllabus. If you successfully complete Task 1, you will earn one extra point on the first quiz.
2. *Task 2: Give me data*: Go to **Discussions** on **Blackboard**. Click on **Content Forum**. I have started a thread called **Data for Day 1**. Please answer the three questions that I have asked in this thread. If you successfully complete Task 2 by 9:00 a.m. on Tuesday, January 15th, then you will earn one extra point on the first exam.

The questions that I have asked:

1. Have you ever completed an online/hybrid course? (Respond with yes or no.)
2. If you have completed an online/hybrid course, rank your experience with this course on a scale of 1 to 4, where 1 = poor, 2 = fair, 3 = good, and 4 = excellent. Provide a very brief explanation for your ranking (one sentence at most). If you have not completed an online/hybrid course, respond n/a for not applicable.
3. How many semesters have you completed at this university?

Reproduced with permission from Alison Kelly.

Box 13.1). Asking students in that email to visit your course website or LMS site, complete a task, and come prepared with something before the first face-to-face class is a great way to test your students' literacy with the online components of the course. You might consider having them post something to a discussion board, download the syllabus, read and take a syllabus quiz, or any other task that gets students engaged with the online tools you are using.

Welcome Video Script

Providing students with a welcome video for your course is another great way to enhance your social presence (see Chapter 8) from the beginning of the course. The following questions can help to get you started in scripting your video.

- What is the purpose of the video?

- What information about the course would you like to share with your students in the video?

- Are there any technologies that you would like to introduce to students in the video?

- Are there any tasks that you want to instruct students to do after the video is complete?

- How will you tell students about the video (i.e., via email, posting an announcement on the LMS site)?

TABLE 13.1.
Video Chronology Template

0:00–0:30
0:30–1:00
1:00–1:30
1:30–2:00
2:00–2:30
2:30–3:00
3:00–3:30
3:30–4:00
4:00–4:30
4:30–5:00

If you have never recorded a video before, scheduling out what you want to say can make sure that the video is both efficient and effective. To hold students' attention, I recommend keeping the first welcome video to no more than five minutes to ensure that students watch the entire video. Table 13.1 offers a video chronology template to help you plan out the content of your welcome video (the timing of the segments can be adjusted as needed). If you find it helpful, draft a script for your video to practice what you will say. If using a script, when it comes time to film, try using talking points rather than reading to the camera.

Tutorials

Depending on the technologies that you have incorporated into your blended course, you might also want to consider offering your students some tutorials or examples of best practices for how to engage with a specific technology or tool. Your institution may also subscribe to online repositories of tutorials (e.g., Atomic Learning: www.atomiclearning.com, or Lynda: www.lynda.com) that you can use within your blended learning environment. If you do not have these resources available, try a general web search to see if a tutorial already exists before creating your own resource (I recommend starting with YouTube).

Checking In

It will be important to touch base with individual students regularly throughout the term to see how the blended environment is working for them. Depending on the size of your course, this can be accomplished in a number of different ways.

Online Discussion Boards

Create an online discussion area for students to dialogue with you about how the course is going. This discussion board can be created so that students can post anonymously or use their names (see more about discussion boards in Chapter 8).

Face-to-Face and Online Office Hours

When students come to visit your face-to-face office hours, make sure to ask questions about the blended course design. You might want to ask how the student is handling the workload, what he or she thinks of specific online tools you have implemented into the course, or if he or she has any questions or needs clarifications about assignments or online activities. If you are conducting online office hours through a chat feature, Skype, Google Hangout, or other means, you can also ask these questions about the blended course design.

Midterm Feedback

At the midpoint of the term, ask students to give you feedback about what is helping and hindering their learning in the course, as well as what general suggestions they have to make the course better for themselves, their peers, and you. If you have specific questions about technologies being used in the course or other elements of the blended course design, you can include these as well. Your LMS may have an online survey tool that can help you collect student feedback anonymously, or you can ask for the feedback during a face-to-face class session.

End-of-Term Evaluations

If you have control over the content for the questions in your end-of-term evaluations, consider adding in a question or two about the blended design elements of the course to gather specific feedback from students. If your end-of-term evaluation is standardized, perhaps you can design a separate informal survey to collect student feedback alongside the more formal instrument.

Email

Depending on their level of experience with the blended modality and the technology tools of your course, students may be emailing you frequently with questions and concerns. If possible, ask your technology department if you can have a separate email account for your blended course to help you manage volume and respond as efficiently as possible. This will be especially helpful if you are teaching multiple sections of the same course and have a large number of students enrolled across sections. Try to keep track of patterns that arise from students' emails and respond to the most frequently occurring questions on the course discussion board or in-class so that students know that you are aware of their concerns.

In-Class Discussion

Let students know that you want them to ask questions or request clarification during in-class time if they need it. The questions that come up could lead to a discussion about the blended design as a whole and help you to make adjustments as needed to help students navigate the course.

Back Channels

If you plan to implement any form of social media into your course, consider also using it for creating discussions with your students about the course elements that are helpful or challenging for them. For example, you could create a Twitter hashtag called #feedback for students to use when offering comments about the blended components of the course. (See Chapter 11 for more on using social media platforms in your course.)

Each of these methods of collecting student feedback about aspects of your blended course design will also foster metacognitive moments for your students as they reflect on what is helping them learn or causing challenges for them in the course. Importantly, if you do not set up specific methods for collecting student feedback about what is going *well* in the course, you may only get communications regarding what is going *poorly*. While knowing what is not working is helpful, having an understanding of the positive elements of the course is also extremely valuable.

Key Ideas From Chapter 13

- All students, particularly those without online or blended learning experience, need to be acculturated to the blended learning environment.
- Welcome emails, videos, and tutorials can help to prepare students for success in your course.
- Despite students' familiarity with a range of technologies, tutorials for tools being used in your blended course may be necessary for student success.
- It is important to create a variety of check-in points to communicate with students throughout the term regarding their experiences in your blended course.

Questions for Faculty

- What are you most concerned about regarding preparing students for success in your course?
- Are you making any assumptions about students' comfort level with technology that may be rooted in misconceptions about students' knowledge regarding particular tools?
- What ideas do you have, other than the ones mentioned in this chapter, to help acculturate students to the blended learning environment and increase their chances of success?
- Does your institution have any supports for student success in blended learning through a tutoring center or other structure?

Questions for Administrators

- What supports for students learning in blended environments are available at your institution?

- What kind of technology support is available for students in blended learning environments? For example, is there a 24-hour help desk for students who may experience problems with the LMS?

Documenting Your Course Design Progress

TABLE 13.2.
Documenting Your Course Design Progress

Course Design Steps	In Your LMS Sandbox
• Complete the "What Do Students Know About Blended Learning?" guiding questions in this chapter. • Decide the various check points you want to include in your course to assess student success in the blended environment and add these to your course map. • Draft a welcome email to your students.	• Design and post a welcome video to your LMS sandbox. • Post a welcome announcement that involves a technology literacy training element. • Create tutorials, either video or text-based, for the most frequently used online components of your course to share with students on or before the first day of class.

NOTES

14

CONCLUSION

Getting Ready to Launch

What Do We Know About Getting Ready to Launch?

Congratulations, you have completed the design for your blended course! You should be well on your way to implementing the course and completing your LMS site. As you prepare to launch the course for the first time, it can be helpful to step back and look at your course design in a holistic way to check the alignment of your goals, objectives, activities, assignments, and assessments. Table 14.1 will walk you through the different components of your blended course design: the syllabus, course organization and design, the activities and assessments, and the student resources and support that you have designed. An additional checklist on accessibility (see Table 14.2) will help you to ensure that all of your course materials and documents are accessible for all learners, including those with sensory disabilities such as hearing or visual impairments. There is room for comments on each of the checklists if you need to follow-up on an item or ask for help from your academic technology unit, disciplinary department, disability services office, or another support unit on your campus.

A Step-by-Step Guide for Getting Ready to Launch

Blended Course Implementation Checklist

Ensuring Accessibility in Blended Courses Checklist
Ensuring that the blended course you create is accessible for all learners is crucial. Table 14.2 offers a checklist that will help you methodically review all of the technological components of your course documents and LMS site to ensure their accessibility. For additional support with online accessibility, I highly recommend Coombs (2010).

TABLE 14.1.
Blended Course Implementation Checklist

Instructor: _____ Dept: _____

Course: _____

The following should be present in all blended courses:

	Yes	No	Comments
Syllabus			
The students have easy digital access to a course syllabus that provides information that the students need to know about the course prior to the first meeting	☐	☐	
The intended outcomes of the course (goals and objectives) are clearly stated in the syllabus *QM	☐	☐	
The course syllabus adheres to University policies (i.e., academic misconduct, disability, etc.)	☐	☐	
The course syllabus includes the instructor's policy for communicating with students that states the turn-around time for email and phone responses	☐	☐	
The course syllabus states minimal technology requirements for the course	☐	☐	
Course Organization and Design			
The instructor has drafted an email to students at the beginning of the class letting them know where to go and how to access the course	☐	☐	
A welcome announcement is posted on the opening page of the course; instructions there clearly indicate how the student should get started	☐	☐	
An orientation is included to familiarize the students with course components and their location in the course	☐	☐	
Navigation throughout the online component of the course is well organized to ensure students will be able to find resources as needed *QM	☐	☐	
"Netiquette" expectations for all components of the online course communication components are posted or stated in the syllabus *QM	☐	☐	
The syllabus or course description includes minimum technical skills expected for student success *QM	☐	☐	
Descriptive words or phrases are used for hyperlinks instead of general phrasing such as "click here" *QM	☐	☐	
The links and course media function properly	☐	☐	
Interactive technologies work correctly	☐	☐	
Term-specific course data are correct	☐	☐	
What students need to complete for the face-to-face and online components of the course are clearly outlined *QM	☐	☐	

(Continues)

TABLE 14.1. *(Continued)*

	Yes	No	Comments
Activities and Assessment			
The content of the course and the learning activities chosen allow students to successfully complete the intended outcomes for the course *QM	☐	☐	
The learning activities foster interaction between the student and the course materials	☐	☐	
Social presence has been designed into the course activities to ensure communication among students and between students and the instructor *QM	☐	☐	
Rubrics or other assessment criteria have been provided so that students know how their work will be evaluated *QM	☐	☐	
There are a range of different assessments, including formative and summative, throughout the course *QM	☐	☐	
The assessments are aligned with the intended outcomes for the course *QM	☐	☐	
The assessments are aligned with the course learning activities and content so that student learning is scaffolded and supported *QM	☐	☐	
All materials and resources used in the course have appropriate citations, if needed *QM	☐	☐	
Student Resources and Support			
Students have ready access to the required technologies for the course	☐	☐	
Instructions on accessing and using the technologies in the course are sufficient and easy to understand	☐	☐	
Technical support and troubleshooting information for the LMS or other online course tools is made available to the students *QM	☐	☐	
Tutoring information is available for students to access in the course	☐	☐	
Library information is available for students to access in the course if the library is being used for course resources	☐	☐	
There is a course evaluation plan built into the course to collect student feedback.	☐	☐	
Total Number of Guidelines		/30	

Adapted from North Virginia Community College Technology Applications Center (2011).

*QM refers to a component that aligns with a "Quality Matters" standard (see www.qmprogram.org). More information about QM is included in Chapter 7.

TABLE 14.2.
Checklist of Best Practices for Ensuring Accessibility in Blended Courses

Instructor: _____ Dept: _____

Course: _____

The following should be present in all blended courses:

	Yes	No	Comments
Before the Course Begins			
The students have been provided with your course textbook/media requirements before the class starts	☐	☐	
You have contacted the Office of Disability Services to discuss your use of multimedia tools before you decide to implement them	☐	☐	
You have listed the Office of Disability Services statement on your syllabus	☐	☐	
You have provided students with the URL for accommodations in your LMS	☐	☐	
Course textbooks were selected at least six weeks prior to the start of the semester and posted online for students to see	☐	☐	
Textbook information includes the correct ISBN number and edition to be used; if electronic copies are mentioned, they correspond to the paper version	☐	☐	
When possible, you have chosen materials from publishers and journals that provide electronic content	☐	☐	
Textbooks have been made available at the library reserves desk	☐	☐	
LMS			
The syllabus is provided in a Word format	☐	☐	
If you include links on your LMS pages, they have accompanying text that has a meaningful description	☐	☐	
Buttons in your LMS menu have descriptive text	☐	☐	
If your LMS page includes redirects or timed actions (e.g., clicking OK to continue), provide adequate response time for users of screen readers or users with mobility impairments	☐	☐	
If your LMS site includes timed actions (e.g., quizzes), ensure that you can adjust response time if needed	☐	☐	
Type styles, sizes, and orientations are consistent throughout your LMS (HINT: consider using the preset Styles function)	☐	☐	
Color combinations are used that provide sufficient contrast between foreground and background	☐	☐	
You have avoided flickering texts or animations	☐	☐	
For HTML table-based layouts, provide appropriate headers and data call designations	☐	☐	

(Continues)

TABLE 14.2. *(Continued)*

	Yes	No	Comments
Acronyms and abbreviations are spelled out (screen readers pronounce these as single words)	☐	☐	
Auditory and Visual Content			
The preset "Styles" feature in Word has been used to apply headers to all documents	☐	☐	
There are no ornate fonts (HINT: use sans serif fonts such as Verdana)	☐	☐	
Headers are larger font sizes than the body of the text	☐	☐	
No fonts are smaller than 10-point font	☐	☐	
1.5 spacing is used when possible	☐	☐	
For documents over six pages in length, a table of contents has been created (HINT: use "References" tab in Word)	☐	☐	
All images, graphs, and figures have alt Text tags (HINT: right click on image, select format picture, and click on alt text)	☐	☐	
All tables have clear labels for rows and columns and no empty cells	☐	☐	
No documents have been "Saved as Web"	☐	☐	
All hyperlinks have been added using the "Insert Hyperlink" feature and all hyperlinks are spelled out in the text	☐	☐	
All tables have row and column headings	☐	☐	
All graphs have alt Text tags (HINT: right click on image, select format picture, and click on alt text)	☐	☐	
Color and highlighting are not the only means of providing information	☐	☐	
Excel worksheets are labeled appropriately (not just Sheet 1 or Sheet 2)	☐	☐	
All words in a PDF can be individually highlighted with your cursor (i.e., the text will not be read as a picture; when in doubt, create a text-only HTML version of the content)	☐	☐	
All Word documents have been made accessible before conversion to PDF	☐	☐	
"Tag" PDF documents whenever possible; for specific instructions visit AccessAbility: http://accessibility.psu.edu/pdf/	☐	☐	
PDFs that cannot be made accessible have been provided in an alternative format, such as an HTML page, Word file, or RTF file; alternative files are posted alongside PDFs	☐	☐	
No text files with multiple columns have been converted to PDFs (screen readers might still read the text across columns)	☐	☐	
ALT (Alternative Text) tags have been used on all visual elements including charts, graphs, mathematical/scientific notation, photos, and so on (HINT: right click on image, select format picture, and click on alt text)	☐	☐	

(Continues)

TABLE 14.2. *(Continued)*

	Yes	No	Comments
Extended text descriptions are provided for all complex images including charts, graphs, mathematical/scientific notation, photos, and so on	☐	☐	
All PowerPoint slides have simple layouts and avoid busy, themed backgrounds	☐	☐	
Content of PowerPoint slides is organized in a logical structure	☐	☐	
Fonts for PowerPoint slides are larger than 14-point font and a sans serif font (e.g., Verdana) is used	☐	☐	
Color combinations in PowerPoint presentations are used that provide sufficient contrast between foreground and background	☐	☐	
Ample white space is provided on each PowerPoint slide	☐	☐	
All audio narrations of PowerPoint slides discuss the slide's content in relation to the larger themes or ideas of the course	☐	☐	
A transcript of narration for each PowerPoint slide has been added to the notes section of that slide	☐	☐	
There are no PowerPoint slide transitions or automatic timing functions used	☐	☐	
Slides have been designed with a slide layout format provided in the software	☐	☐	
Captioning or written transcripts have been provided for all video or audio files	☐	☐	
Video files are embedded into one of the following players: QuickTime, RealPlayer, iTunes, YouTube	☐	☐	
Videos with visual information critical to comprehension include a description of events or images	☐	☐	
Written descriptions are provided for all content offered in a flash file	☐	☐	
All Flash content is accessible; for more information, see: www .adobe.com/accessibility/products/flash/author/html	☐	☐	

Reproduced with permission from Kirsten Behling.

Key Ideas From Conclusion

- When you have completed your course design, it is important to look at the blended course you have created in its entirety to see whether it is aligned in the way that you intended.
- Comprehensive checklists can help you ensure that the course is student-centered and accessible for all learners.

Questions for Faculty

- What kind of quality assurance process do you have for the blended courses at your institution?
- Does your institution employ checklists similar to the ones used in this chapter?

Questions for Administrators

- What kind of quality assurance process do you have for the blended courses at your institution?
- Does your institution employ checklists similar to the ones used in this chapter? If not, do you want to create them as a resource for faculty developing blended courses?

Documenting Your Course Design Progress

TABLE 14.3.
Documenting Your Course Design Progress

Course Design Steps	In Your LMS Sandbox
- Complete the "Blended Course Implementation Checklist" to self-assess your course design progress. - Complete the "Checklist of Best Practices for Ensuring Accessibility in Blended Courses" to self-assess the accessibility of your blended course components. - Celebrate! You've worked hard to design this blended course!	- Check all links and components of your LMS sandbox to ensure they are functional. - Consider having a student enroll in the LMS sandbox to explore the online environment and offer feedback before the official launch of the course.

NOTES

GLOSSARY

Accessibility: the ability for students with diverse abilities to access all course content (Chapter 4, Chapter 9, and Conclusion)

Active Learning: a method of teaching through which students learn by doing (Chapter 5)

Alignment: the process through which course goals, learning objectives, assignments, activities, and assessments are intentionally connected to support student learning and success (Chapter 6)

Analytic Rubric: a form of rubric that breaks down what is being evaluated into specific parts to assess them individually (Chapter 3)

Analytics: data on student learning, available through a Learning Management System (LMS), that can help to measure student participation in online components such as discussion boards, whether students watch videos, how long students spend on the LMS website, and other pieces of information (Introduction and Chapter 4)

Andragogy: teaching methods and strategies used with and for adult learners (Chapter 1)

App: mini software applications on mobile devices that are designed to complete a specific task or function (Chapter 11)

Assessment: the process of communicating clear, measurable, and observable objectives for student learning and gathering data and evidence to ensure that those objectives have been met (Chapter 3)

Asynchronous: interacting online at different times than other users, such as through a discussion board (Chapter 7)

Backward Design: an approach to compiling a course that starts with the desired results for student learning (Chapter 1)

Blended Learning: a course modality that replaces face-to-face components with online tools and content delivery in an intentional design that promotes active and self-directed learning (Introduction; see also, Hybrid Learning)

Blog: a "web log" where authors can post ideas or content on a particular topic (Chapter 4 and Chapter 11)

Bloom's Taxonomy: a taxonomy of learning broken into six stages of cognitive development (Chapter 2)

Classroom Assessment Technique (CAT): a kind of formative feedback that includes a range of techniques and strategies (Chapter 3)

Collaborative Learning: a form of group work in which students work together, although not necessarily interdependently, to accomplish the same goal (Chapter 5)

Cooperative Learning: a form of group work in which students work together interdependently to accomplish the same goal (Chapter 5)

Copyright: a form of protection for an original work that offers the originator or another party the right to reproduce the work (Chapter 9)

Creative Commons: a form of copyright licensing that includes six different options for sharing work; each license is denoted by a symbol that can be added to a print work, web resources, or other creation (Chapter 9)

Direct Instruction: primarily instructor-led learning where students depend on the instructor for information or instructions to move forward; common forms are a face-to-face lecture, a video lecture, or a video tutorial (Chapter 1, Chapter 5, and Chapter 6)

Discussion Board: a common LMS feature that allows instructors to create conversation threads for students to interact with asynchronously (Chapter 8)

F2F: a short hand for "face-to-face" components of a blended course (Chapter 6)

Flipped Classroom: a model of blended learning in which course content is delivered online so that more active learning such as group work, discussion, or presentations can take place in the face-to-face classroom (Introduction and Chapter 5)

Formative Feedback: information collected on student learning that is often ungraded, low-stakes, and efficient; the feedback can inform instructor's strategies moving forward in the course as well as help students to gauge their own learning in real time (Chapter 3)

Goal: what students will know or understand upon successful completion of a course (Chapter 2)

Guided Inquiry: primarily student-led learning where students autonomously explore course materials with only minimal instructions or direction from the instructor (Chapter 1, Chapter 5, and Chapter 6)

Holistic Rubric: a form of rubric that looks at what is being evaluated as a whole (Chapter 3)

Hybrid Learning: a course modality that replaces face-to-face components with online tools and content delivery in an intentional design that promotes active and self-directed learning (Introduction; see also, Blended Learning)

Hyperlink: a link from one location or document to another by clicking on a highlighted piece of text or an image (Chapter 12 and Conclusion)

Learning Management System (LMS): a software system that offers an organization structure for a range of course tools to be used by both groups and individuals over the Internet (also called "Course Management System" or "E-Learning Platform"); LMSs typically include a suite of tools designed to deliver, track, report on, and manage learning content, learner progress, and learner interactions (Chapter 7)

Lecture Capture: software that allows you to record images from your computer screen such as a PowerPoint or website demonstration into a video format (Chapter 10; see also, Screen Capture)

LibGuide: a set of webpages that librarians create to help their patrons with research, learning more about a particular topic, or to integrate into a particular course or assignment (Chapter 9)

Metacognition: the process of intentionally reflecting on one's own learning (Chapter 3, Chapter 5, Chapter 6, and Chapter 13)

Midterm Feedback: the process of collecting information at midterm to assess the level of student learning in a course (Chapter 3 and Chapter 13)

Multimedia: resources that combine both words and pictures; common examples are videos, interactive textbooks, or online simulations (Chapter 10)

Objective: what students will be able to do upon successful completion of a course (Chapter 2; see also, Outcome)

Online Learning: environments where learning occurs primarily online through synchronous and asynchronous learning tools (Introduction)

Open Educational Resource (OER): educational materials that are available for public use, including courses, textbooks, videos, assessment tools, or other materials (Chapter 9)

Outcome: a stated objective for what a student will be able to do upon successful completion of a course (Chapter 2; see also, Objective)

Pedagogy: teaching methods and strategies used with and for learners who are children (Chapter 1)

Podcast: primarily audio recordings that can also include video; podcasts are easily transferable to mobile devices (Chapter 10)

Problem-Based Learning (PBL): a form of group work in which students seek out information and work together to solve a real-world problem and present their findings to others (Chapter 5)

Publisher Resources: online materials that can be purchased along with a course textbook such as flashcards, problem sets, case studies, videos, or other content that is digitally based (Chapter 4 and Chapter 9)

Quality Matters (QM): a continuous improvement rubric model for assuring the quality of online courses through a faculty-driven, collegial peer review process (Chapter 7 and Conclusion)

Rubric: a tool used to evaluate the learning objectives for a particular assignment or project (Chapter 3)

Scaffolding: breaking down or "chunking" a project or set of information into smaller pieces that build on one another for easy completion or consumption by learners (Chapter 3)

Screen Capture: software that allows you to record images from your computer screen such as a PowerPoint or website demonstration into a video format (Chapter 10; see also, Lecture Capture)

Social Media: web-hosted spaces where people connect to share information and collaborate on ideas; common social media platforms are Twitter and Facebook (Chapter 11)

Social Presence: intentional activities and elements of the online environment that ask students to communicate and interact with the instructor or their peers (Chapter 8)

Summative Feedback: information collected on student learning that is often evaluative in nature, graded, and high-stakes; examples include projects, exams, reports, and papers (Chapter 3)

Syllabus: a permanent record of a course that serves a range of purposes for instructors, students, and administrators (Chapter 12)

Synchronous: interacting online simultaneously in real time, such as through a chat feature or web conferencing tool (Chapter 7)

Team-Based Learning (TBL): a form of group work in which students work together in self-managed teams to solve problems (Chapter 5)

Tutorial: a form of instruction meant to teach students how something works (Chapter 10, Chapter 11, Chapter 13)

Universal Design for Learning: a set of principles used to ensure accessibility for a diverse set of learners, including learners with disabilities (Introduction)

Wiki: a collaborative learning tool where multiple users can contribute to creating a space simultaneously; a popular example is Wikipedia (Chapter 4, Chapter 7, and Chapter 11)

APPENDIX A

Purposes of Syllabi References

Syllabus Purpose	References
As a contract or legal document	Bers, Davis, & Taylor, 1996; Eberly, Newton, & Wiggins, 2001; Doolittle & Lusk, 2007; Matejka & Kurke, 1994; Parkes & Harris, 2002; Wasley, 2008
As a permanent record	Eberly, Newton, & Wiggins, 2001; Parkes & Harris, 2002
As a resource for student learning	Eberly, Newton, & Wiggins, 2001; Estes, 2007; Grunert, 1997; Haebanek, 2005; Matejka & Kurke, 1994; Parkes & Harris, 2002
As a motivational tool	Estes, 2007; Harris, 1993; Slattery & Carlson, 2005
As an interaction tool	Armstrong, 2011; Cummings, Bonk, & Jacobs, 2002
As a collaboration tool	DiClementi & Handelsman, 2005; Hudd, 2003
As a socialization tool	Collins, 1997; Estes, 2007; Sulik & Keys, 2014; Wesp, Kash, Sandry, & Patton, 2013
As a communication tool	Altman & Cashin, 1992; Eberly, Newton, & Wiggins, 2001; Hammons & Shock, 1994; Matejka & Kurke, 1994; Smith & Razzouk, 1993; Thompson, 2007
As an interpersonal tool	Baecker, 1998; DiClementi & Handelsman, 2005; Eberly, Newton, & Wiggins, 2001; Harnish & Bridges, 2011; Harnish, O'Brien McElwee, Slattery, Frantz, Haney, Shore, & Penley, 2011; Ishiyama & Hartlaub, 2002; Thompson 2007
As an administrative tool	Bers, Davis, & Taylor, 1996; Cullen & Harris, 2009; Eberly, Newton, & Wiggins, 2001; Palmer, Bach, & Streifer 2014
As a course or curriculum development tool	Eberly, Newton, & Wiggins, 2001; Palmer, Bach, & Streifer 2014
As a professional development tool	Albers, 2003; Bers, Davis & Taylor, 1996; Millis, 1989
As a marketing tool	Thompson, 2007

APPENDIX B

Syllabi Content Area References

Content Area	References
Instructor Information	Altman & Cashin, 1992; Appleby, 1994; Collins, 1997; Doolittle & Siudzinski, 2010; Hammons & Shock, 1994; Matejka & Kurke, 1994; Parkes & Harris, 2002; Slattery & Carlson, 2005
Course Information	Altman & Cashin, 1992; Appleby, 1994; Doolittle & Siudzinski, 2010; Hammons & Shock, 1994; Matejka & Kurke, 1994; Parkes & Harris, 2002
Course Description	Appleby, 1994; Doolittle & Siudzinski, 2010; Hammons & Shock, 1994; Slattery & Carlson, 2005
Course Rationale	Hammons & Shock, 1994; Slattery & Carlson, 2005
Pedagogical Methods or Instructional Techniques	Hammons & Shock, 1994; Matejka & Kurke, 1994
Readings/Materials and Textbooks	Altman & Cashin, 1992; Appleby, 1994; Collins, 1997; Doolittle & Siudzinski, 2010; Hammons & Shock, 1994; Matejka & Kurke, 1994; Parkes & Harris, 2002; Slattery & Carlson, 2005
Goals and Objectives	Altman & Cashin, 1992; Appleby, 1994; Doolittle & Siudzinski, 2010; Hammons & Shock, 1994; Matejka & Kurke, 1994; Parkes & Harris, 2002; Slattery & Carlson, 2005
Calendar/Course Schedule	Altman & Cashin, 1992; Appleby, 1994; Collins, 1997; Doolittle & Siudzinski, 2010; Hammons & Shock, 1994; Matejka & Kurke, 1994; Parkes & Harris, 2002; Slattery & Carlson, 2005
Course Policies	Altman & Cashin, 1992; Collins, 1997; Doolittle & Siudzinski, 2010; Hammons & Shock, 1994; Matejka & Kurke, 1994; Parkes & Harris, 2002
Assignments	Collins, 1997; Doolittle & Siudzinski, 2010; Hammons & Shock, 1994; Matejka & Kurke, 1994; Slattery & Carlson, 2005
Grading Procedures	Altman & Cashin, 1992; Appleby, 1994; Collins, 1997; Doolittle & Siudzinski, 2010; Hammons & Shock, 1994; Matejka & Kurke, 1994; Parkes & Harris, 2002; Slattery & Carlson, 2005
Support Services or Student Resources	Altman & Cashin, 1992; Collins, 1997; Doolittle & Siudzinski, 2010; Slattery & Carlson, 2005

APPENDIX C

Syllabus Examples

Syllabus 1

Economics/College of Arts and Sciences

STATS250: Applied Statistics   Spring 2013, Syllabus

Part 1: Course Information

Instructor Information
Instructor: Alison Kelly
Email: professor@institution.edu (email is the best way to reach me; I will try to respond within 24 hours M–F)
Phone: (555) 555-5555

Office: Building location

Office Hours: Tuesdays and Thursdays in my office from 3:00 pm–4:30 pm

Course Information
Face-to-Face Meetings: Tuesdays 10:00 a.m.–11:15 a.m.
Location: Archer 349

Catalog Description: Application of statistical analysis to real-world business and economic problems. Topics include data presentation, measures of central locations and dispersion, probability and probability distributions, estimation and hypothesis testing, simple and multiple regression models. The use of Excel is emphasized throughout the course.

Prerequisites: MATH130, MATH134, MATH146, or MATH165; ability to use and have regular access to a computer.

Credit Hours: 4.0
This course follows the Federal Government's Credit Hour definition: "An amount of work represented in intended learning outcomes and verified by evidence of student achievement that is an institutional established equivalence that reasonably approximates no less than:

1. One hour of classroom or direct faculty instruction and a minimum of two hours of out of class student work each week for approximately 15 weeks for one semester or trimester hour of credit, or 10 to 12 weeks for one quarter hour of credit, or the equivalent amount of work over a different amount of time; or

2. At least an equivalent amount of work as required in paragraph (1) of this definition for other academic activities as established by the institution including laboratory work, internships, practica, studio work, and other academic work leading to the award of credit hours."

Course Context

This course follows a ***hybrid format*** where the majority of the lectures are covered outside of class time. Class time is used to review the more difficult concepts and solve homework exercises and case studies. In-class and out-of-class requirements are as follows:

- In-class requirements: A weekly, 1.5-hour, in-class meeting where we review the weekly-assigned material and solve homework exercises and case studies. Students also take quizzes and exams during this time period (1.5 hours a week).
- Out-of-class requirements: Outside of class, students are required to complete assigned readings, watch video lectures, complete conceptual exercises (referred to as LearnSmart) and online homework assignments (10.5 hours a week).

The total time required per week is a minimum of 12 hours.

Instructional Materials Plan

1. **Required Textbook**: *Business Statistics—Communicating with Numbers,* by Sanjiv Jaggia and Alison Kelly, 2013, McGraw-Hill Publishers **WITH** McGraw-Hill's CONNECT (online assignment and assessment system). Choose one of the following options:

   a. eBook with CONNECT: Purchase CONNECT Plus from website

   b. New textbook packaged with CONNECT. Available at bookstore. After purchase, go to website and enter access code for CONNECT found on textbook.

   c. Used textbook and CONNECT purchased separately. Purchase CONNECT from website

Unless you are given a used text, the eBook with CONNECT is the most economical way to purchase the class materials. No matter which option you choose, after a one-time log in for CONNECT, you will be able to access all online components for the class directly from Blackboard.

2. Online lectures on selected topics will be available on Blackboard.

3. Prior to each class meeting, students will be required to answer a set of conceptual exercises using LearnSmart (a component of CONNECT—it is an adaptive self-study technology). Each LearnSmart assignment must be submitted **before** the scheduled class meeting time. Late submissions are not allowed. These assignments evaluate the student's work in preparation for the class meeting.

4. Students will be required to complete weekly online homework assignments using CONNECT. These homework assignments are typically due within 48 hours after each face-to-face meeting. CONNECT grades homework automatically and provides feedback on any problems that students are challenged to solve. Late submissions are not allowed.

5. There will be approximately five unannounced quizzes during class meetings.

6. There will be two scheduled exams and final.

Technology Requirements
- Internet connection (DSL, LAN, or cable connection desirable)
- Access to Blackboard
- Access to CONNECT
- Access to Microsoft Excel 2007 or 2010. I expect that you have had some exposure to Excel

Blackboard Access
To access this course on Blackboard you will need access to the Internet and a supported Web browser (Internet Explorer, Firefox, Safari). To ensure that you are using a supported browser and have required plug-ins, see the Supported Browsers link for your Blackboard course.

Technical Assistance
If you need technical assistance at any time during the course or to report a problem with Blackboard you can:

- Visit Blackboard's FAQ's Webpage
- Visit Blackboard's Student's Webpage
- Submit a Problem Ticket

Part 2: Course Goals & Learning Objectives

Goals	Objectives	Assessments
Upon successful completion of this course, students will be able to do the following:	*Upon successful completion of this course, students will be able to do the following:*	*Students will be assessed on the following learning objectives:*
Understand how to summarize data	1. Present data effectively with the use of tables and graphs. 2. Compute and interpret measures of central location and measures of dispersion.	On-line assignments, in-class assignments, in-class quizzes and exams
Understand probability and probability distributions	1. Employ basic concepts including conditional probabilities and rules of probabilities. 2. Compute summary measures for a probability distribution. 3. Compute probabilities for discrete and continuous probability distributions. 4. Discuss the sampling distribution of the sample mean and the sample proportion.	On-line assignments, in-class assignments, in-class quizzes and exams
Understand statistical inference	1. Construct confidence intervals for the population mean and the population proportion. 2. Select a sample size to estimate the population mean and the population proportion. 3. Conduct hypothesis tests about a population mean and population proportion.	On-line assignments, in-class assignments, in-class quizzes and exams
Understand regression analysis	1. Interpret the components of a regression model. 2. Use the regression model to make a prediction using sample data. 3. Assess the regression model.	On-line assignments, in-class assignments, in-class quizzes and exams

Part 3: Grading and Course Policies

Graded Course Activities

- **LearnSmart assignments** contribute **10%** to the final grade. These assignments **must be submitted BEFORE the scheduled meeting time**. The grade evaluates your work on the material as a part of the required preparation to the class meeting. Visit the Connect: LearnSmart folder under Course Documents on Blackboard for all of these assignments.
- **On-line homework assignments** contribute **20%** to the final grade. These assignments require submitting written solutions on CONNECT at or before the due date. Visit the Connect: Homework folder under Course Documents on Blackboard for all of these assignments.
- **Participation** contributes 5% to final grade. In addition to having opportunities during every in-class meeting, you have the opportunity to participate in two online forums; one addresses technology issues (visit the Technology Forum under **Discussions** on **Blackboard**) and the other addresses content issues (visit the Content Forum under **Discussions** on **Blackboard**).
- **In-class quizzes** contribute **5%** to final grade.
- **Two exams** contribute **15% each** to the final grade.
- **Final Exam (cumulative)** contributes **30%** to the final grade.

Activity	*Contribution to Final Grade*
LearnSmart	10%
On-line homework assignments	20%
Participation	5%
In-class quizzes	5%
Two in-class exams	15% (each)
Final exam	30%

Late Work Policy

- *No* make-ups are given on any quiz/exam and no late assignments are accepted. Unexcused absences will result in a zero for that particular quiz/exam. For an absence to be excused, you must come see me during my office hours and explain your absence (documentation always helps). I will reweight your grade **after** this occurs.

Viewing Grades in Blackboard

All grades will be available via the Grade Center on Blackboard. Please consider the online gradebook as a courtesy to you, subject to errors given various upgrades and shifts in the software. I reserve the right to make gradebook corrections to keep it consistent with the syllabus so that your grade reflects true performance, not software or user error. If you see something that doesn't make sense, please alert me! Thanks much for your help.

Letter Grade Assignment

Final grades assigned for this course will be based on the percentage of total points earned and are assigned as follows:

> 92% A	76%–78% C+
89%–92% A-	73%–75% C
86%–88% B+	69%–72% C-
83%–85% B	50%–68% D range
79%–82% B-	< 50% F

Academic Integrity Policy

Academic dishonesty (cheating, plagiarism, etc.) will be reported to the Office of Student Affairs. Reports will be addressed through the Student Discipline System. An undergraduate student who has been found to have violated this policy is subject to an automatic grade of "F" in the course and to suspension, enforced withdrawal, or dismissal from the University or appropriate lesser penalties if warranted by the circumstances.

Disability Statement

If you anticipate issues related to the format or requirements of this course, please meet with me. I would like us to discuss ways to ensure your full participation in the course. If you determine that formal, disability-related accommodations are necessary, it is very important that you be registered with the Office of Disability Services (123 University Street, 4th floor, 555-555-5555) and notify me of your eligibility for reasonable accommodations. We can then plan how best to coordinate your accommodations.

The Early Alert Project

This class participates in Suffolk's Early Alert Project. Around week 6, I will notify the Ballotti Learning Center if you have struggled with writing or language skills, excessive absences, incomplete work, or difficulty with the course content. This warning is not an official grade, yet it indicates concerns I have about your progress that need to be addressed immediately. If you are contacted about an Early Alert, please respond to those individuals and also visit me during my office hours so we may talk about strategies for how you can be successful in this class.

Outside of Class Resources

Students are strongly recommended to meet with me in person or contact me via email with any questions or for help in understanding the material and solving problems. In addition, the Ballotti Learning Center provides <u>free</u> STATS250 study sessions and individual tutoring (visit the Ballotti website for more information).

<u>Miscellaneous</u>

- In the event that the university cancels classes, such as for severe weather, students are expected to continue with readings and homework as originally scheduled. Any change in the due dates of readings/assignments will be posted on the Announcement page on Blackboard.
- The schedule, policies, procedures, and assignments in this course are subject to change in the event of extenuating circumstances, by mutual agreement, and/or to ensure better student learning. It is the student's responsibility to check the Announcement page on Blackboard for corrections or updates to the syllabus.

Part 4: Topic Outline/Schedule

<u>Prior to each in-class meeting</u>, you are expected to:

- Complete all relevant readings,
- View online lectures (see Blackboard > Course Documents > Video folder), and
- Complete LearnSmart assignments (see Blackboard > Course Documents > CONNECT: LearnSmart folder).

<u>Within 48 hours of each in-class meeting</u>, you are expected to:

- Complete online homework assignment (see Blackboard > Course Documents > CONNECT: Homework Assignments folder).

Date	Assignment
Week 1: 1/15, Tuesday	**First in-class meeting:** Prior to class, complete two tasks outlined on Blackboard's Announcement Page.
Week 2: Prior to 1/22, Tuesday	**Read** Chapter 1: Statistics and Data 1.1 The Relevance of Statistics 1.2 What Is Statistics? 1.3 Variables and Scales of Measurement **Watch** Module 1. Statistics and Data **Complete** LearnSmart Chapter 1.

Date	Assignment
	Read Chapter 2: Tabular and Graphical Methods
	2.1 Summarizing Qualitative Data 2.2 Summarizing Quantitative Data
	Watch Module 2. Tabular and Graphical Methods
	Complete LearnSmart Chapter 2.
1/22, Tuesday	**In-class meeting** on Chapter 1: Sections 1.1–1.3 and Chapter 2: Sections 2.1–2.2.
1/24, Thursday	**Submit** Homework Assignment 1 and Homework Assignment 2 by 10 a.m.
Week 3: Prior to 1/29, Tuesday	**Read** Chapter 3: Numerical Descriptive Measures 3.1 Measures of Central Location 3.2 Percentiles and Boxplots 3.4 Measures of Dispersion 3.6 Analysis of Relative Location 3.7 Summarizing Grouped Data
	Watch Module 3. Numerical Descriptive Measures
	Complete LearnSmart Chapter 3.
1/29, Tuesday	**In-class meeting** on Chapter 3: Sections 3.1–3.2, 3.4, 3.6–3.7.
1/31, Thursday	**Submit** Homework Assignment 3 by 10 a.m.
Week 4: Prior to 2/5, Tuesday	**Read** Chapter 4: Introduction to Probability 4.1 Fundamental Probability Concepts 4.2 Rules of Probability 4.3 Contingency Tables and Probabilities
	Watch Module 4. Introduction to Probability
	Complete LearnSmart Chapter 4.
2/5, Tuesday	**In-class meeting** on Chapter 4: Sections 4.1–4.3.
2/7, Thursday	**Submit** Homework Assignment 4 by 10 a.m.

Date	Assignment
Week 5: Prior to 2/12, Tuesday 2/12, Tuesday 2/14, Thursday	**Read** Chapter 5: Discrete Probability Distributions 5.1 Random Variables 5.2 Expected Value and Variance 5.3 The Binomial Distribution 5.4 The Poisson Distribution **Watch** Module 5. Discrete Probability Distributions **Complete** LearnSmart Chapter 5. **In-class meeting** on Chapter 5: Sections 5.1–5.4 **Submit** Homework Assignment 5 by 10 a.m.
Week 6:	****** In-class Exam 1: Tuesday, February 19th: Chapters 1–5******
Week 7: Prior to 2/26, Tuesday 2/26, Tuesday 2/28, Thursday	**Read** Chapter 6: Continuous Probability Distributions 6.1 Continuous Random Variables and the Uniform Distribution 6.2 The Normal Distribution 6.3 Solving Problems with Normal Distributions **Watch** Module 6. Continuous Probability Distributions **Complete** LearnSmart Chapter 6. **In-class meeting** on Chapter 6: Sections 6.1–6.3. **Submit** Homework Assignment 6 by 10 a.m.
Week 8: Prior to 3/5, Tuesday 3/5, Tuesday 3/7, Thursday	**Read** Chapter 7: Sampling and Sampling Distributions 7.1 Sampling 7.2 The Sampling Distribution of the Sample Mean 7.3 The Sampling Distribution of the Sample Proportion **Watch** Module 7. Sampling and Sampling Distributions **Complete** LearnSmart Chapter 7. **In-class meeting** on Chapter 7: Sections 7.1–7.3 **Submit** Homework Assignment 7 by 10 a.m.

Date	*Assignment*
Week 9: Prior to 3/19, Tuesday	**Read** Chapter 8: Estimation 8.1 Interval Estimators 8.2 Confidence Interval for the Population Mean when σ is known 8.3 Confidence Interval for the Population Mean when σ is unknown 8.4 Confidence Interval for the Population Proportion 8.5 Selecting the Required Sample Size **Watch** Module 8. Estimation **Complete** LearnSmart Chapter 8
3/19, Tuesday	**In-class meeting** on Chapter 8: Sections 8.1–8.4
3/21, Thursday	**Submit** Homework Assignment 8 by 10 a.m.
Week 10: Prior to 3/26, Tuesday	**Read** Chapter 9: Hypothesis Testing 9.1 Introduction to Hypothesis Testing 9.2 Hypothesis Test of the Population Mean when σ is known **Watch** Module 9. Hypothesis Testing (Part 1) **Watch** Module 10. Hypothesis Testing (Part 2) **Complete** LearnSmart Chapter 9 (Parts 1 and 2)
3/26, Tuesday	**In-class meeting** on Chapter 9: Sections 9.1–9.2
3/28, Thursday	**Submit** Homework Assignment 9 by 10 a.m.
Week 11: Prior to 4/2, Tuesday	**Read** Chapter 9: Hypothesis Testing 9.3 Hypothesis Test of the Population Mean when σ is unknown 9.4 Hypothesis Test of the Population Proportion **Watch** Module 11. Hypothesis Testing (Part 3) **Complete** LearnSmart Chapter 9 (Part 3)
4/2, Tuesday	**In-class meeting** on Chapter 9: Sections 9.3–9.4
4/4, Thursday	**Submit** Homework Assignment 9 by 10 a.m.
Week 12:	*** **In-class Exam 2: Tuesday, April 9th: Chapters 6–9*****

Date	Assignment
Week 13: Prior to 4/16, Tuesday	**Read** Chapter 14: Basics of Regression Analysis 14.1 The Simple Linear Regression Model 14.2 The Multiple Linear Regression Model 14.3 Goodness-of-Fit Measures **Watch** Module 12. Basics of Regression Analysis **Complete** LearnSmart Chapter 14
4/16, Tuesday	**In-class meeting** on Chapter 14: Sections 14.1–14.3.
4/18, Thursday	**Submit** Homework Assignment 10 by 10 a.m.
Week 14: Prior to 4/23, Tuesday	**Read** Chapter 15: Inference with Regression Models 15.1 Tests of Significance **Watch** Module 13. Tests of Individual Significance **Complete** LearnSmart Chapter 15 **In-class meeting** on Chapter 15: Section 15.1.
4/23, Tuesday 4/25, Thursday	**Submit** Homework Assignment 11 by 10 a.m.
*** In-class Final, Wednesday, May 1st, 3:20 pm–5:10 pm: Chapters 1–9, 14, 15***	

Syllabus 2

Bio 105-A: Humans and the Evolutionary Perspective
Dr. Eric W. Dewar
Email: professor@institution.edu • *phone:* (555) 555-5555
on twitter: @twitterhandle
Office: Building Location • *lab:* Building Location
Office Hours: Monday, Wednesday 1:00 p.m.–2:00 p.m and Friday 10:00 a.m.–11:00 a.m.

Spring 2015 lecture schedule

Legend for schedule:
F2F = **Face-to-face meeting agenda**
M = **Instructional module**: Complete the modules and any readings before your F2F meeting.
P = **Project**: The fieldwork for these assignments is scheduled during those weeks.
D = **Discussion/response readings**: 500-word responses are due by class time on the day that we will discuss the article or chapter.

Week	Topic	Out-of-Class Work	F2F Meeting	What's Due
0	Getting acclimated to working online	M0: Pre-class orientation to online resources		Print syllabus, make online profile
1	From natural philosophy to biology	M1: Evolution before Darwin M2: Earth history	Course welcome and overview	
2	Phylogenies	M3: Working with fossils M4: The tree of life D1: Derry, 1999	Science as a process	Response 1
3	Variation	P1: The comparative method M5: Cellular basis of variation	Data collection at Museum of Comparative Zoology	
4	Natural Selection	M6: Hypothesizing natural selection P1: Video demo of evolutionary tree software M7: Genes as Historians	Group meetings about project	

Week	Topic	Out-of-Class Work	F2F Meeting	What's Due
5	Historical pattern of evolution	M8: Adaptations	Molecules versus morphology	Preliminary comparative method results
6	Darwin in the *Origin*	D2: Darwin, 1859 M9: Speciation	Darwin in the *Origin*	Response 2 Comparative method project
7	The human career	M10: Coevolution M11: Becoming human D3: Jablonski & Chaplin, 2010	Skin color in humans	Response 3
8	Sex, love, etc.	M12: Animal sociality M13: Sex and whatnot D4: Leidy, 2012	Menopause—adaptive or not?	Response 4
9	Dr. Darwin	M14: Selection and disease M15: Human dysevolution D5: Curtis et al., 2011	What is disgusting?	Response 5
10	Alternatives to evolution	M16: Finding alternatives to evolution D6: Intelligent Design as an alternative?	The creation-evolution debate in the United States	Response 6
11	Unique humanness?	M17: The evolutionary perspective D7: Fitch, 2002	Why are we musical?	Response 7
12	Finals week			*Cambridge Companion* chapter response

Course information for Bio 105-A

Class times & location

F2F meetings Monday, Wednesday, or Friday at 11:00 a.m.–11:50 a.m. in Archer 561

Online coursework will be linked through Blackboard

Data collection will take place in Cambridge, accessible by public transportation.

Catalog description

BIO 105 (4 cr.)—Major topics include the scientific basis of evolution, the fossil history of vertebrates, evidence of evolution in the human body, and applying an evolutionary perspective to the social interactions and possible futures of humanity. Meets one of the non-laboratory science requirements for the non-science major. This reading and writing intensive course is a non-laboratory science option for non-science majors. This course will not fulfill requirements for a major or a minor in Biology. Usually offered fall of odd years and each summer.

Course goals and learning objectives

Goals	Objectives	Assessments
Upon successful completion of this course, students will:	*Upon successful completion of this course, students will be able to:*	*How the student will be assessed on these learning objectives:*
1. Understand the historical development of evolutionary theory as an example of the process of science.	A. Compare the worldviews of natural philosophy and science.	F2F discussion
	B. Relate technological advances to increases in knowledge.	F2F discussion
2. Understand the evidence of evolution.	A. Describe the actions of genes (and proteins) in living things and how they are inherited.	Quizzes, project, and F2F discussion
	B. Describe historical outcomes such as biodiversity and biogeography.	Quizzes, project, and F2F discussion
	C. Compare processes and outcomes in the history of life to illustrate general evolutionary trends.	Quizzes, project, written responses, and F2F discussion

Goals	Objectives	Assessments
Upon successful completion of this course, students will:	*Upon successful completion of this course, students will be able to:*	*How the student will be assessed on these learning objectives:*
	D. Comparative human characteristics to appreciate their inheritance from our vertebrate ancestors, and how these attributes affect our bodies, minds, and societies.	Quizzes, project, written responses, and F2F discussion
	E. Critique scientific ideas and one's own presuppositions rigorously, both in writing and discussion.	Quizzes, written responses, and discussion
3. Value biological novelty and uniqueness.	A. Develop an appreciation for the interconnectedness and contingency of the natural world.	F2F discussion and participation in F2F meetings
4. Understand the goals and work of scientists.	A. Differentiate between public opinion and scientific consensus.	Written responses and F2F discussion
	B. Test hypotheses through observation in natural history museums and the environment.	Fieldwork project
5. Identify sources of information about biological topics.	A. Frame one's personal insights about novel ideas in writing and discussion.	Written responses and F2F discussion

This course follows the Federal Government's Credit Hour definition: "An amount of work represented in intended learning outcomes and verified by evidence of student achievement that is an institutional established equivalence that reasonably approximates no less than:

1. One hour of classroom or direct faculty instruction and a minimum of two hours of out of class student work each week for approximately fifteen weeks for one semester or trimester hour of credit, or ten to twelve weeks for one quarter hour of credit, or the equivalent amount of work over a different amount of time; or
2. At least an equivalent amount of work as required in paragraph (1) of this definition for other academic activities as established by the institution including laboratory work, internships, practica, studio work, and other academic work leading to the award of credit hours."

Course materials

Required text: Carl Zimmer (2010) *The Tangled Bank: An Introduction to Evolution.* Roberts and Company Publishers (ISBN-13 978-0981519470).

Admission fees: You will be responsible for admission fees at Boston-area museums and National Park Service locations.

Other assigned readings and class resources will be linked to the Blackboard, Sawyer Library, and iTunesU sites.

Communication: All students <u>must</u> have a working Suffolk email address and access to Blackboard and the Suffolk e-library site. Use of Twitter is optional but encouraged.

Readings, quizzes, formal writing, and discussion

This is a course about thinking. We write in order to clarify our ideas so that we may use them in discussion with one another. Throughout the semester, I want to challenge you to integrate the new scientific content you encounter with your existing knowledge—from your major, your earlier schooling, and the wider world around you.

Quizzes in lecture modules

Short quizzes will follow each lecture module on the Blackboard site. Each of these will be worth 10 points. These quizzes will be in multiple-choice format and short-essay format. You may use the text when taking the quizzes. The quizzes will cover the major ideas of the modules or readings. Each quiz must be completed on the first attempt. If you have technical difficulties with completing a quiz, then please contact me by email. Each quiz will be available until class time of the day that a chapter's content is to be worked with. I will drop the lowest two scores.

Comparative method project

This project is intended to get you thinking with the comparative method. For this assignment you will go to the Museum of Comparative Zoology at Harvard University in order to collect data to build your own evolutionary trees. Your work with data collection and evolutionary tree generation will be discussed in a paper that will be about 1500 to 2000 words in length. Details are forthcoming on Blackboard.

Response papers on discussion readings

The nine articles in the lecture schedule will become the basis for discussions in class. A meaningful response should describe and elaborate on one new insight you gained from the reading. A good response will justify your insight based on information from the reading, the text, or other sources such as previous experience or coursework. A response should *not* merely be a summary of the reading or just enumerate what you found confusing. Each response should be about 500 words in length. The responses, worth 20 points each, will be evaluated on the basis of the depth of the insight and the clarity with which you justify your conclusions from the reading. See examples of good responses on the course Blackboard page.

All documents should be submitted by class time via the "Safe Assignment" link for each response on the course's Blackboard site. Late assignments will not be accepted because the discussions will take place on the day that a response is due. Writing a response after the discussion has happened defeats the purpose of the assignment, which is to crystallize one's thoughts about a novel topic *before* class so that you can use those ideas in discussion.

Discussion of articles in class and with Twitter

I score each student's participation in discussion on a 0–3 scale: 3 = clearly understood the reading and actively contributed ideas to the discussion, including responding to others' ideas; 2 = understood the reading and made some contribution to the discussion; 1 = present but did not speak; 0 = absent from class on a discussion day. These scores are turned into a percentage of 27 points (9 discussions × 3 points possible for each) and included in the following grading scheme.

This semester you may participate in the discussion via Twitter to **@DewarLabSU** or using the hashtag **#subio105**. I will keep a window open for this stream during lecture for questions as well as for letting students respond to ideas in discussion. Feel free to respond to one another vocally or via the Twitter stream.

Outside of class time, that Twitter feed will aggregate news about evolution that is relevant or of interest to our group. You may post to that user as well if you find other relevant articles.

Final paper

By the ninth week of class, I would like for you to choose a chapter to write about from the *Cambridge Companion to the "Origin of Species"*, which is available from the Sawyer Library's website (and via our Blackboard page). Darwin's work is analyzed from different scientific angles and extended to consider its impact with respect to literature, politics, religion, and other fields of human inquiry. The final paper will be a beefed-up response (1200–1500 words) to one of those chapters; an excellent response would be one that addresses the ideas of your chapter and ties it to knowledge from this course, your major, and/or other personal interests.

Course grading will be based on:

Percentage of best 5 scores on 7 written responses to readings	200 pts.
Comparative method project	100 pts.
Module quizzes and other assignments	200 pts.
Participation in class discussion	100 pts.
Final paper	50 pts.
Final grade is a percentage of	650 pts.

Course policies

Communication

All students <u>must</u> have a working Suffolk email address and access to Blackboard. Please refer to the University website for support or visit the Help Desk in Sawyer. Access to Twitter and iTunesU among other resources is also expected.

Blackboard, ebrary, and iTunes U

The course site on Blackboard will link to many required materials for the course, instructions and guidance about assignment, and helpful online resources—very few paper documents will be distributed this semester. I will also use the class list on Blackboard or from the Registrar to send and archive most course announcements, so check your email often. The Suffolk library's ebrary site will contain some required readings, but I will link to them through our Blackboard site.

Attendance policy

Students will be responsible for satisfying all course objectives whether present in class or not. Those absent on the day of lecture should get notes from students who were in class. Any points for discussion participation will be lost due to absence. Excessive absence or lateness will result in a penalty on the final course grade.

Class cancellation

If Suffolk classes are cancelled on the day that a quiz or discussion was scheduled and a response was due, they will happen on the next scheduled class day. In that event, watch for an email with clarification.

Academic dishonesty

I take academic dishonesty very seriously, particularly for students who wish to enter a field with explicit ethical guidelines. Cheating on examinations, plagiarism and/or improper acknowledgment of sources in essays or research papers, and the use of a single essay or paper in more than one course without the permission of the instructor constitute unacceptable academic conduct. Student work may be checked by plagiarism-detection software.

Students will be held to the guidelines explained in the Student Policy and Procedures Handbook. All cases of plagiarism, cheating, and other forms of academic dishonesty will be dealt with severely by the dean of students, in accordance with page 17 of the Handbook. Academic dishonesty will be reported to the Office of Student Affairs. Reports will be addressed through the Student Discipline System. An undergraduate student who has been found to have violated this policy is subject to an automatic grade of "F" in the course and to suspension, enforced withdrawal, or dismissal from the University or appropriate lesser penalties if warranted by the circumstances.

APPENDIX D

Weekly Course Design Task List

Chapter	Topic	Course Design Steps	In Your LMS Sandbox
1	Fundamentals of Blended Teaching and Learning	• Based on what you have read in this chapter, use Table 1.2 to reflect on the similarities and differences between traditional courses you have taught and what you envision for your blended course. • Complete an interview with an experienced blended course instructor to see what advice he or she can offer as you begin the blended course design process. • Explore the pedagogical and andragogical principles in your own teaching using Table 1.3. • If you will be redesigning a previously taught course, gather all of your course materials in one place (physically or digitally) for easy reference.	• Establish an LMS sandbox space to work in through your institution's academic computing or instructional design office.
2	Writing Course Goals and Learning Objectives	• Find a copy of your department's program goals and/or discuss the alignment of the program goals and your course with your department chair. • Brainstorm the essential questions for your course. • Decide whether your course will have technology-specific learning objectives. • Complete an initial draft of your course goals and learning objectives.	• Think about how and where you plan to communicate your course goals and learning objectives to students in your LMS sandbox.

Chapter	Topic	Course Design Steps	In Your LMS Sandbox
3	Assessing Student Learning in Your Blended Course	• Using the reflection questions in this chapter, consider which assessments will best measure student learning in your blended course. • Using Table 3.3, decide which of your assignments will be fully online, fully in-class, or a mix of both online and in-class components. • Map the major assignments for your course using Table 3.4. • Complete Table 3.5 to map out your formative and summative assessments in a weekly schedule. • Apply the checklist in Table 3.6 to your course assessment plan. • Review the overall assessment plan and how it relates to your course goals using Table 3.7. • Create the assignments and assessments from Table 3.4 and Table 3.5. • Create rubrics, as appropriate, for your assignments using the tools and templates provided.	• Build an assignment in your LMS sandbox (there may be a special tool for this). • Find out if your LMS has a rubric tool and decide whether you plan to use it within your course. • Begin to explore the Grade Book function included in your LMS and find out if there are training opportunities or online resources to learn how to use this tool.
4	Online Assessment Tools	• Decide whether you plan to use online assessment tools within your course. • For any online assessment tools you choose to use, create a troubleshooting guide for students. • Think about how you will talk with students about your expectations for online assessments to ensure students will understand what constitutes cheating or academic dishonesty. • Consider whether and how you will collect feedback from students regarding their perceptions of what cheating means in an online environment.	• If you plan to use specific online assessment tools, contact your academic computing office to explore how the tools can be integrated within your LMS. • In your sandbox, set up the online assessment tools so that you can test the tools to ensure they are working as you intend. • Post any troubleshooting guides that you create for students in your LMS sandbox.

Chapter	Topic	Course Design Steps	In Your LMS Sandbox
		• Review the activities from Chapter 3 and add in any additional notes based on what you have learned from Chapter 4.	• If you decide to collect feedback from students using an online survey, create that survey in your LMS sandbox.
5	Designing Effective Learning Activities	• Use Table 5.3 to list the direct instruction and guided inquiry activities you have previously used. • Answer the reflective questions provided throughout the chapter to identify additional learning activities to include in your course. • Use Table 5.4 and Table 5.5 to categorize your learning activities as face-to-face, online, or both.	• Create a list of the online learning activities you have identified in this chapter that will need to be incorporated into your LMS sandbox (this list can be reviewed when you read Chapter 7).
6	Mapping Your Blended Course	• Locate all holidays, exams, and other important dates and count the weeks and course days available in the term that you will be teaching your blended course. • Begin to fill out the blended course map template in Table 6.3 with the elements of your course that you have already planned and keep the course map handy for when you need to add additional components after completing future workbook chapters. • Complete the reflective questions to consider while course mapping to help self-assess the course map as you create it. • Consider which elements of your course map you might want to include in your syllabus schedule (this will help you prepare for Chapter 12).	• Find out if your LMS has a calendar tool and decide whether you plan to use it within your course to help students remember due dates and deadlines. • Wait until your course map is complete and solidified before building your LMS site structure; it may be difficult to make changes throughout the site later on if you move assignments to another week or rearrange learning objectives.

Chapter	Topic	Course Design Steps	In Your LMS Sandbox
7	Getting to Know Your LMS	• Choose which LMS components you plan to include in your blended course. • Use Table 7.6 to map out the content areas for your LMS site. • Find out if there are best practice design resources for your LMS; these resources might be institution-specific or through your LMS provider. • Review the work you have completed for previous chapters to see what might pertain to what you have learned in this chapter regarding your LMS.	• Decide the structure for your LMS navigation menu. • Based on the map you created in Table 7.6, begin to create the content areas for your blended course on the LMS site. • Explore the aesthetic choices available within your LMS including text color, "theme" options, and icon possibilities. • Review the work you have completed for previous chapters to see what you can add to your LMS site given what you have learned in this chapter.
8	Creating Social Presence in Your Blended Course	• Add to your blended course map (started in Chapter 6) with the components of social presence that you plan to include in the course each week. • Establish expectations for yourself about the frequency of communications you plan to have with students using online tools. • Consider how to manage student expectations of your online social presence; is this something that you will discuss with them face-to-face or include in your syllabus?	• Add separate feedback discussion boards in your LMS to collect student questions about technology and content. • Add a discussion board in your LMS for students to introduce themselves to one another. • Create a space for students to have "off-topic" conversations.
9	Finding Resources Online	• Explore the publisher resources available for your course to see if there are any that might be appropriate to include.	• Explore the tools available in your LMS for creating "Learning Modules," a tool that can offer a helpful structure for organizing different pieces of course content including OERs.

Chapter	*Topic*	*Course Design Steps*	*In Your LMS Sandbox*
		• Complete the "Online Resources Scavenger Hunt" included in this chapter to find already-existing multimedia that relates to your course content. • Use Table 9.1 to develop a potential list of OERs that might be appropriate to include in your course. • Assess the list you created in Table 9.1 using the checklist in Table 9.2. • Schedule an appointment with your disability services office to ensure that any OERs that you choose for your course are accessible for all students.	• If appropriate for your course, create a Learning Module on a topic of your choice using the tool in your LMS • Using the list you created in Table 9.1. and that you assessed with Table 9.2, begin integrating OERs, library material, or publisher resources that are most. appropriate for your course into your LMS.
10	Creating Multimedia Resources	• Outline and record a short lecture video for your course using the template provided to see if video lectures might be a component you want to include in your course. • Check to see what campus resources are available to ensure the best production quality for your multimedia resources. • Ask around to see if colleagues in your department have created multimedia resources; what campus or online resources did they find to be the most helpful?	• Explore the different technologies available at your institution for video creation and lecture capture. • Choose a technology platform for creating videos in your blended course. • Create a lecture video and post within your LMS sandbox. • Create and post supplementary resources for video lectures or podcasts so that your students can actively engage with the multimedia resources (see Chapter 5 for more on designing effective learning activities).
11	Mobile Devices, Apps, and Social Media	• Identify learning objectives where mobile devices or social media could enhance the learner experience.	• If you will be using apps or social media in your course, add links to these components to your LMS sandbox.

Chapter	Topic	Course Design Steps	In Your LMS Sandbox
		• Using Table 11.1, decide if you will be using any apps or social media in your blended course. • If you will be using apps or social media in your course, add descriptions or instructions about these components to your course syllabus.	• Consider making a tutorial video for the app or social media platform that you choose to integrate into your course and adding this tutorial to your LMS sandbox.
12	The Blended Course Syllabus	• Choose the components that you will include in your blended course syllabus and make a note of any modifications that might need to be made because of the blended modality. • Check to see if your campus has a syllabus template that is recommended for traditional, blended, or online courses. • Ask around to see if there are other instructors of blended courses who might be willing to share an example of their syllabus with you. • Begin drafting your blended course syllabus, adding in components that you have already designed from previous workbook activities. • Gather campus-specific resources and support structures to include in your syllabus (e.g., the help desk number for LMS-related questions).	• Create a space for your course syllabus in your LMS sandbox navigation menu. • Upload your completed syllabus to your LMS site. • If you plan to have students complete a syllabus quiz, design the quiz in your LMS and place a link to the quiz in the same content area that you post the syllabus.
13	Preparing Your Students for Success	• Complete the "What Do Students Know About Blended Learning?" guiding questions in this chapter. • Decide the various check points you want to include in your course to assess student success in the blended environment and add these to your course map.	• Design and post a welcome video to your LMS sandbox. • Post a welcome announcement that involves a technology literacy training element.

Chapter	Topic	Course Design Steps	In Your LMS Sandbox
		• Draft a welcome email to your students.	• Create tutorials, either video or text-based, for the most frequently used online components of your course to share with students on or before the first day of class.
14	Getting Ready to Launch	• Complete the "Blended Course Implementation Checklist" to self-assess your course design progress. • Complete the "Checklist of Best Practices for Ensuring Accessibility in Blended Courses" to self-assess the accessibility of your blended course components. • Celebrate! You've worked hard to design this blended course!	• Check all links and components of your LMS sandbox to ensure they are functional. • Consider having a student enroll in the LMS sandbox to explore the online environment and offer feedback before the official launch of the course.

APPENDIX E

Sample Timed Test Help Document

Created by Pat Hogan for SCI 171, Suffolk University, and reproduced with permission.

The following are some software issues that may impact your ability to take timed tests on Blackboard. If you are using your own laptop, please go to the Helpdesk and have them check your computer for compatibility issues.

Things to Do Before the Test

Proactively checking on these items may make the test experience more positive.

Browser: Blackboard works best with Firefox. If you are using your own computer and do not have Firefox installed, install it. If you do not know how to install it, talk to the Helpdesk.

Old Blackboard Settings: Some Blackboard settings do not impact your ability to view lectures or other materials but may impact your ability to access and submit the exam during a timed test. If you have not updated any of your Blackboard settings (how you access Blackboard) on your computer for some time, you might need to do that. Again, visit Helpdesk.

Older Versions of Other Software Applications: You may need to update programs like Java—talk to the Helpdesk.

Wireless Connection: If you are using a wireless connection and know that there is a possibility it may become unstable (home wireless system, coffee shop wireless system), then *do not* take your test at that location. Students have reported no problem with the campus wireless connections (e.g., Sawyer Library) to date.

Blackboard: Blackboard will automatically log you off after three hours if you leave the window open, even if you are not using it. Before the test, log out of Blackboard and then log back in so you know that it will not log off during the test. If for some reason you do get logged off, log back in promptly because the test timer continues to run when you are logged off.

Other Open Applications: Close out as many open applications as you can prior to starting the exam. Having many windows open may cause instabilities that lead to exam access or application problems. Keep your computer workspace clean during the exam.

Things to Do During the Test

You can take the exam as many times as you wish during the 80-minute period. I have not instituted a one-time only submit exam because students accidentally submitted the exam before they completed it. Note that the exam resets when you retake it. You will not be given an indication about which problems you got wrong on your previous attempts.

Timer Stops: If the timer stops during the test, that is an indication to you that the Blackboard access is in fail mode. Note any answers you have already inputted and restart the exam. If you are denied access to Blackboard after this occurs, email me and include your hybrid number so I know where to look.

Error Message Upon Submission: If you get a Blackboard screen with a red warning that denies you access upon submission, your Blackboard connection is in fail mode.

Forced Save: I have instituted a Forced Save at the end of the testing period so when the test is over, whatever your last completed attempt is, that will be saved. I did this because students went up to the wire, did not save their exam before the exam timed out, and lost their work.

Proctoring: I am online and monitoring my email for questions and problems. You may get an email from me during the exam on clarifying an exam question or some other topic related to the exam.

Things To Do After the Test

Do not panic. If technical issues prevented your successful completion of the exam, we will work to get you in the right situation so you can complete the exam successfully.

REFERENCES

Abel, R. (2005). *Achieving success in internet-supported learning in higher education: Case studies illuminate success factors, challenges, and future directions.* Lake Mary, FL: The Alliance for Higher Education Competitiveness, Inc. Retrieved from http://www.a-hec.org/research/study%5Freports/IsL0205/TOC.html

Abeysekera, L., & Dawson, P. (2015). Motivation and cognitive load in the flipped classroom: Definition, rationale and a call for research. *Higher Education Research & Development 34*(1), 1014.

Al-Bahrani, A., & Patel, D. (2015). Incorporating Twitter, Instagram, and Facebook in economics classrooms. *The Journal of Economic Education, 46*(1), 56–67.

Albers, C. (2003). Using the syllabus to document the scholarship of teaching. *Teaching Sociology, 31*(1), 60–72.

Allen, I. E., & Seaman, J. (2007). *Online nation: Five years of growth in online learning.* Needham, MA: Sloan Consortium. Retrieved from http://www.babson.edu/Academics/Documents/babson-survey-research-group/online-nation.pdf.

Allen, I. E., & Seaman, J. (2014). *Grade change: Tracking online education in the United States.* Needham, MA: Babson Survey Research Group and Quahog Research Group.

Alrasheedi, M., Capretz, L. F., & Raza, A. (2015). A systematic review of the critical factors for success of mobile learning in higher education (University Students' Perspective). *Journal of Educational Computing Research, 52*(2), 257–276.

Altman, H. B., & Cashin, W. E. (1992). *Writing a syllabus.* IDEA Paper No. 27. Manhattan, KS: The IDEA Center.

Ambrose, S. A., Bridges, M. W., DiPietro, M., Lovett, M. C., Norman, M. K., & Mayer, R. E. (2010). *How learning works: Seven research-based principles for smart teaching.* San Francisco, CA: Jossey-Bass.

Anderson, L. W., & Krathwohl, D. R. (Eds.). (2001). *A taxonomy for learning, teaching, and assessing: A revision of Bloom's Taxonomy of educational objectives.* New York: Longman.

Angelo, T. A., & Cross, K. P. (1993). *Classroom assessment techniques.* San Francisco, CA: Jossey-Bass.

Appana, S. (2008). A review of benefits and limitations of online learning in the context of the student, the instructor, and the tenured faculty. *International Journal on E-Learning, 7*(1), 5–22.

Appleby, D. C. (1994). How to improve your teaching with the course syllabus. *APS Observer, 7*(3), 18–19, 26.

Armstrong, A. M. (2011). Integrating learning and collaboration using an interactive online course syllabus. In *Proceedings of TCC Worldwide Online Conference 2011* (pp. 10-19). TCCHawaii. Retrieved from https://www.learntechlib.org/j/TCC/v/2011/n/1

Atkins, D., Brown, J. S., & Hammond, A. (2007). A review of the open educational resources (OER) movement: Achievements, challenges, and new opportunities. *Report to The William and Flora Hewlett Foundation.* http://www.hewlett.org/uploads/files/ReviewoftheOERMovement.pdf

Baecker, D. L. (1998). Uncovering the rhetoric of the syllabus: The case of the missing I. *College Teaching, 46*(2), 58–61.

Barczyk, C. C., & Duncan, D. G. (2013). Facebook in higher education courses: An analysis of students' attitudes, community of practice, and classroom community. *International Business and Management, 6*(1), 1–11.

Barkley, E. F., Major, C. H., & Cross, K. P. (2014). *Collaborative learning techniques: A handbook for college faculty.* San Francisco, CA: Jossey-Bass.

Beck, V. (2014). Testing a model to predict online cheating—Much ado about nothing. *Active Learning in Higher Education, 15*(1), 65–75.

Becker, A. H., & S. K. Calhoon. (1999). What introductory psychology students attend to on a course syllabus. *Teaching of Psychology, 26*, 6–11.

Beckett, G. H., Amaro-Jimenez, C., & Beckett, K. S. (2010). Students' use of asynchronous discussions for academic discourse socialization. *Distance Education, 31*(3), 315–335.

Bender, T. (2012). *Discussion-based online teaching to enhance student learning: Theory, practice, and assessment.* Sterling, VA: Stylus.

Berk, R. A. (2009). Multimedia teaching with video clips: TV, movies, YouTube, and mtvU in the college classroom. *International Journal of Technology in Teaching and Learning, 5*(1), 1–21.

Bers, T., Davis, B., & Taylor, B. (2000). The use of syllabi in assessments: Unobtrusive indicators and tools for faculty development. *Assessment Update, 12*(3), 4-7.

Bers, T., Davis, B. D., & Taylor, W. (1996). Syllabus analysis: Are we teaching or telling our students? *Assessment Update, 8*(6), 14–15.

Biggs, J. (1996). Enhancing teaching through constructive alignment. *Higher Education, 32*, 347–364.

Black, E. W., Greaser, J., & Dawson, K. (2008). Academic dishonesty in traditional and online classrooms: Does the "media equation" hold true? *Journal of Asynchronous Learning Networks, 12*(3–4), 23–30.

Blankenship, M. (2011). How social media can and should impact higher education. *Education Digest, 76*(7), 39–42.

Bloom, B. S., & Krathwohl, D. R. (1956). *Taxonomy of educational objectives: The classification of educational goals, by a committee of college and university examiners. Handbook I: Cognitive domain.* New York: Longmans.

Blumberg, P. (2009). Maximizing learning through course alignment and experience with different types of knowledge. *Innovative Higher Education, 34*, 93–103.

Bonwell, C. C., & Eison, J. A. (1991). *Active learning: Creating excitement in the classroom* (ASHE-ERIC Higher Education Report No. 1). Washington, DC: George Washington University.

Borup, J., West, R. E., & Graham, C. R. (2013). The influence of asynchronous video communication on learner social presence: A narrative analysis of four cases. *Distance Education, 34*(1), 48–63.

Bowen, J. A. (2012). *Teaching naked: How moving technology out of your college classroom will improve student learning.* San Francisco, CA: Jossey-Bass.

Brookfield, S. D. (2012). *Teaching for critical thinking: Tools and techniques to help students question their assumptions.* San Francisco, CA: Jossey-Bass.

Brothen, T., & Peterson, G. (2012). Online exam cheating: A natural experiment. *International Journal of Instructional Technology and Distance Learning, 9*(2), 15–20.

Burgstahler, S. E. (2008). Universal design of instruction: From principles to practice. In S. E. Burgstahler & R. C. Cory (Eds.), *Universal design in higher education: From principles to practice* (pp. 23–43). Cambridge, MA: Harvard Education Press.

Calhoon, S., & Becker, A. (2008). How students use the course syllabus. *International Journal for the Scholarship of Teaching and Learning, 2*(1), 1–12.

Carmean, C., & Brown, G. (2005). Measure for measure: Assessing course management systems. In P. McGee, C. Carmean, & A. Jafari (Eds.), *Course management systems for learning* (pp. 1–13). Hershey, PA: Information Science Publishing.

Carroll-Barefield, A., Smith, S. P., Prince, L. H., & Campbell, C. A. (2005). Transitioning from brick and mortar to online: A faculty perspective. *Online Journal of Distance Learning Administration, 8*(1). Retrieved from http://www.westga.edu/~distance/ojdla/spring81/carroll81.htm

Caulfield, J. (2011). *How to design and teach a hybrid course.* Sterling, VA: Stylus.

Chen, C. C., & Jones, K. T. (2007). Blended learning vs. traditional classroom settings: Assessing effectiveness and student perceptions in an MBA accounting course. *The Journal of Educators Online, 4*(1), 1–15.

Cheng, A., Jordan, M. E., Schallert, D. L., & The D-Team. (2013). Reconsidering assessment in online/hybrid courses: Knowing versus learning. *Computers & Education, 68,* 51-59.

Christensen, C. M. (2011). *The innovative university: Changing the DNA of higher education from the inside out.* San Francisco, CA: Jossey-Bass.

Christensen, T .K. (2003). Finding the balance: Constructivist pedagogy in a blended course. *The Quarterly Review of Distance Education, 4*(2), 235–243.

Christou, N., Dinov, I. D., & Sanchez, J. (2007, August). Design and evaluation of SOCR tools for simulation in undergraduate probability and statistics courses. *Proceedings of the 56th session of the International Statistical Institute meeting, Lisbon, Portugal.* Retrieved from http://www.stat.auckland.ac.nz/~iase/publications/isi56/IPM40_Christou.pdf.

Clark, R. C., & Mayer, R. E. (2008). *E-learning and the science of instruction: Proven guidelines for consumers and designers of multimedia learning.* San Francisco, CA: Pfeiffer.

Clark, W., Logan, K., Luckin, R., Mee, A., & Oliver, M. (2009). Beyond web 2.0: Mapping the technology landscapes of young learners. *Journal of Computer Assisted Learning, 25*(1), 56–69.

Collins, A., & Halverson, R. (2009). *Rethinking education in the age of technology: The digital revolution and schooling in America.* New York: Teachers College Press.

Collins, T. (1997). For openers . . . An inclusive course syllabus. In W. Campbell & K. Smith (Eds.), *New Paradigms for College Teaching* (pp. 79–102). Edina, MN: Interactive Books.

Collison, G., Elbaum, B., Haavind, S., & Tinker, R. (2000). *Facilitating online learning: Effective strategies for moderators.* Madison, WI: Atwood Publishing.

Coombs, N. (2010). *Making online teaching accessible: Inclusive course design for students with disabilities.* San Francisco, CA: Jossey-Bass.

Cullen, R., & Harris, M. (2009). Assessing learner-centeredness through course syllabi. *Assessment & Evaluation in Higher Education, 34,* 115–125.

Cummings, J. A., Bonk, C. J., & Jacobs, F. (2002). Twenty-first century college syllabi: Options for online communication and interactivity. *Internet and Higher Education, 5*(1), 1–19.

Davidson, N., & Major, C. H. (2014). Boundary crossings: Cooperative learning, collaborative learning, and problem-based learning. *Journal on Excellence in College Teaching, 25*(3–4), 7–55.

Davidson, N., Major, C. H., & Michaelsen, L. K. (Eds.). (2014). Small group learning in higher education—cooperative, collaborative, problem-based, and team-based learning [Special issue]. *Journal on Excellence in College Teaching, 25*(3–4).

De George-Walker, L., & Keefe, M. (2010). Self-determined blended learning: A case study of blended design. *Higher Education Research, 29*(1), 1–13.

DeLozier, S. J., & Rhodes, M. G. (2016). Flipped classrooms: A review of key ideas and recommendations for practice. *Educational Psychology Review*, 1–11. doi 10.1007/s10648-015-9356-9

DiClementi, J. D., & Handelsman, M. M. (2005). Empower students: Class-generated course rules. *Teaching of Psychology, 32*, 18–21.

Diemer, T. T., Fernandez, E., & Streepey, J. W. (2012). Student perceptions of classroom engagement and learning using iPads. *Journal of Teaching and Learning with Technology, 1*(2), 13–25.

Doolittle, P. E., & Lusk, D. L. (2007). The effects of institutional classification and gender on faculty inclusion of syllabus components. *Journal of Scholarship and Teaching and Learning, 7*(2), 62–78.

Doolittle, P. E., & Siudzinski, R. A. (2010). Recommended syllabus components: What do higher education faculty include in their syllabi? *Journal of Excellence in College Teaching, 20*(3), 29–61.

Doyle, T. (2011). *Learner-centered teaching: Putting the research on learning into practice.* Sterling, VA: Stylus.

Dray, B. J., Lowenthal, P. R., Miszkiewicz, M. J., Ruiz-Primo, M. A., & Marczynski, K. (2011). Developing an instrument to assess student readiness for online learning: A validation study. *Distance Education, 32*(1), 29–47.

Du, C. (2011). A comparison of traditional and blended learning in introductory principles of accounting course. *American Journal of Business Education, 4*(9), 1–10.

Duch, B. J., Groh, S. E., & Allen, D. E. (Eds.). (2001). *The power of problem-based learning: A practical "how to" for teaching undergraduate courses in any discipline.* Sterling, VA: Stylus.

Eberly, M. B., Newton, S. E., & Wiggins, R. A. (2001). The syllabus as a tool for student-centered learning. *The Journal of General Education, 50*(1), 56–74.

Estes, T. (2007). Constructing the syllabus: Devising a framework for helping students learn to think like historians. *History Teacher, 40*(2), 183–201.

Everson, M., Gundlach, E., & Miller, J. (2013). Social media and the introductory statistics course. *Computers in Human Behavior, 29*(5), A69–A81.

Field, S., Sarver, M. D., & Shaw, S. F. (2003). Self-determination: A key to success in postsecondary education for students with learning disabilities. *Remedial and Special Education, 24*(6), 339–349.

Fink, L. D. (2003). *Creating significant learning experiences: An integrated approach to designing college courses.* San Francisco, CA: Jossey-Bass.

Fink, S. B. (2012). The many purposes of course syllabi: Which are essential and useful? *Syllabus, 1*(1), 1–12.

Forehand, M. (2005). Bloom's taxonomy: Original and revised. In M. Orey (Ed.), *Emerging perspectives on learning, teaching, and technology.* Retrieved from http://projects.coe.uga/edu/epltt/

Garrison, D. R. (2011). *E-learning in the 21st century: A framework for research and practice* (2nd ed.). New York: Routledge.

Garrison, D. R., Anderson, T., & Archer, W. (2000). Critical inquiry in a text-based environment: Computer conferencing in higher education. *The Internet and Higher Education*, *2*(2), 87–105.

Garrison, D. R., & Kanuka, H. (2004). Blended learning: Uncovering the transformative potential in higher education. *The Internet and Higher Education*, *7*(2), 95–105.

Garrison, D. R., & Vaughan, N. D. (2008). *Blended learning in higher education: Framework, principles, and guidelines*. San Francisco, CA: Jossey-Bass.

Getzel, E. E. (2008). Addressing the persistence and retention of students with disabilities in higher education: Incorporating key strategies and supports on campus. *Exceptionality: A Special Education Journal*, *16*(4), 207–219.

Gikas, J., & Grant, M. M. (2013). Mobile computing devices in higher education: Student perspectives on learning with cellphones, smartphones & social media. *Internet and Higher Education*, *19*, 18–26.

Glazer, F. S. (Ed.). (2012). *Blended learning: Across the disciplines, across the academy*. Sterling, VA: Stylus.

Graham, C. R., Woodfield, W., & Harrison, J. B. (2013). A framework for institutional adoption and implementation of blended learning in higher education. *Internet and Higher Education*, *18*, 4–14.

Graham, M. (2014). Social media as a tool for increased student participation and engagement outside the classroom in higher education. *Journal of Perspectives in Applied Academic Practice*, *2*(3), 16–24.

Graham-Matheson, L., & Starr, S. (2013). Is it cheating or learning the craft of writing? Using Turnitin to help students avoid plagiarism. *Research in Learning Technology*, *21*, 1–13.

Grunert, J. (1997). *The course syllabus: A learning centered approach*. Bolton, MA: Anker Publishing.

Gunawardena, C. N. (1995). Social presence theory and implications for interaction and collaborative learning in computer conferences. *International Journal of Educational Telecommunications*, *1*(2), 147–166.

Gunawardena, C. N., & Zittle, F. J. (1997). Social presence as a predictor of satisfaction within a computer-mediated conferencing environment. *American Journal of Distance Education*, *11*(3), 8–26.

Gurell, S. (2008). *Open educational resources handbook*. Center for Open and Sustainable Learning. Retrieved from http://wikieducator.org/OER_Handbook/educator_version_one.

Guy, R. (2012). The use of social media for academic practice: A review of literature. *Kentucky Journal of Higher Education Policy and Practice*, *1*(2), 7.

Haebanek, D. V. (2005). An examination of the integrity of the syllabus. *College Teaching*, *53*(2), 62–64.

Hall, H., & Davison, B. (2007). Social software as support in hybrid learning environments: The value of the blog as a tool for reflective learning and peer support. *Library and Information Science Research*, *29*, 163–187.

Hammons, J. O., & Shock, J. R. (1994). The course syllabus reexamined. *Journal of Staff, Programming, & Organizational Development*, *12*(1), 5–17.

Harnish, R. J., & Bridges, R. K. (2011). Effect of syllabus tone: Students' perceptions of instructor and course. *Social Psychological Education*, *14*, 319–330.

Harnish, R. J., O'Brien McElwee, R., Slattery, J. M., Frantz, S., Haney, M. R., Shore, C. M., & Penley, J. (2011). Creating the foundation for a warm classroom climate: Best practices in syllabus tone. *APS Observer*, *24*, 23–27.

Harris, M. M. (1993). Motivating with the course syllabus. *National Teaching and Learning Forum, 3*(1), 1–3.

Harris Poll. (2014). *Pearson student mobile device survey.* Pearson. Retrieved from http://www.pearsoned.com/wp-content/uploads/Pearson-HE-Student-Mobile-Device-Survey-PUBLIC-Report-051614.pdf.

Heer, R. (2011). *A model of learning objectives. Based on* A taxonomy for learning, teaching, and assessing: A revision of Bloom's taxonomy of educational objectives. Ames, IA: Center for Excellence in Learning and Teaching, Iowa State University. Retrieved from http://www.celt.iastate.edu/wp-content/uploads/2015/09/RevisedBloomsHandout-1.pdf

Hensley, G. (2005). Creating a hybrid college course: Instructional design notes and recommendations for beginners. *Journal of Online Learning and Teaching, 1*(2), 1–7.

Hmelo-Silver, C. E. (2004). Problem-based learning: What and how do students learn? *Educational Psychology Review* 16(3): 235–266.

Hofstein, J. D., Tucker, L., Swarner, K., Moriarty, D., Tegas, L., DeMarte, N., & Adiletta, N. (2013). Using iPads in the chemistry classroom: Focusing on paperless education and identification and directed use of pedagogically directed applications. *The Chemical Educator, 18*, 248–254.

Hudd, S. S. (2003). The syllabus under construction: Involving students in the creation of class assignments. *Teaching Sociology, 31*(2), 195–202.

Hung, M., Chou, C., Chen, C., & Own, Z. (2010). Learner readiness for online learning: Scale development and student perceptions. *Computers & Education, 55*(3), 1080–1090.

Ishiyama, J. T, & Hartlaub, S. (2002). Does the wording of syllabi affect course assessment in introductory political science classes? *Political Science and Politics, 35*(3), 567–570.

Johnson, L., Adams Becker, S., Estrada, V., & Freeman, A. (2014). *NMC horizon report: 2014 higher education edition.* Austin, TX: The New Media Consortium.

Johnson, L., Adams Becker, S., Estrada, V., & Freeman, A. (2015). *NMC horizon report: 2015 higher education edition.* Austin, TX: The New Media Consortium.

Jones, I. S., Blankenship, D., & Hollier, G. (2013). Am I cheating? An analysis of online students' perceptions of their behaviors and attitudes. *Psychology Research, 3*(5), 261–269.

Joosten, T. (2012). *Social media for educators: Strategies and best practices.* San Francisco, CA: Jossey-Bass.

Jusoff, K., & Khodabandelou, R. (2009). Preliminary study on the role of social presence in blended learning environment in higher education. *International Education Studies, 2*(4), 79.

Kelley, D. H., & Gorham, J. (1988). Effects of immediacy on recall of information. *Communication Education, 37*(3), 198–207.

Kember, D., McNaught, C., Chong, F. C. Y., Lam, P., & Cheng, K. F. (2010). Understanding the ways in which design features of educational websites impact upon student learning outcomes in blended learning environments. *Computers & Education, 55*, 1183–1192.

Kilmon, C., & Fagan, M. H. (2007). Course management software adoption: A diffusion of innovations perspective. *Campus-Wide Information Systems, 24*(2), 134–144.

Kim, H. K. (2011). Promoting communities of practice among non-native speakers of English in online discussions. *Computer Assisted Language Learning, 24*(4), 353–370.

King, C., & So, K. K. F. (2014). Creating a virtual learning community to engage international students. *Journal of Hospitality & Tourism Education, 26*, 136–146.

Knowles, M. S. (1980). *The modern practice of adult education: From pedagogy to andragogy* (revised and updated). Englewood Cliffs, NJ: Cambridge Adult Education.

Koszalka, T., & Ganesan, R. (2010). Designing online courses: A taxonomy to guide strategic use of features available in course management systems (CMS) in distance education. *Distance Education, 25*(2), 243–256.

Lack, K. A. (2013, March 21). *Current state of research on online learning in postsecondary education.* Retrieved from http://www.sr.ithaka.org/research-publications/current-status-research-online-learning-postsecondary-education.

Laru, J., Näykki, P., & Järvelä, S. (2012). Supporting small-group learning using multiple Web 2.0 tools: A case study in the higher education context. *The Internet and Higher Education, 15*(1), 29–38.

Laster, S., Otte, G., Picciano, A. G., & Sorg, S. (2005, April). *Redefining blended learning.* Presented at the 2005 Sloan-C Workshop on Blended Learning, Chicago, IL.

Lealock, T. L., & Nesbit, J. C. (2007). A framework for evaluating the quality of multimedia learning resources. *Educational Technology & Society, 10*(2), 44–59.

Lehman, R. M., & Conceição, S. C. O. (2010). *Creating a sense of presence in online teaching: How to "be there" for distance learners.* San Francisco, CA: Jossey-Bass.

Loncar, M., Barrett, N. E., & Liu, G. Z. (2014). Towards the refinement of forum and asynchronous online discussion in educational contexts worldwide: Trends and investigative approaches within a dominant research paradigm. *Computers & Education, 73*, 93–110.

LoSchiavo, F. M., & Shatz, M. A. (2011). The impact of an honor code on cheating in online courses. *MERLOT Journal of Online Learning and Teaching, 7*(2), 179–184.

Major, C. H. (2015). *Teaching online: A guide to theory, research, and practice.* Baltimore, MD: Johns Hopkins University Press.

Maki, P. (2010). *Assessing for learning: Building a sustainable commitment across the institution.* Sterling, VA: Stylus Publishing.

Malloy, T. E., & Hanley, G. L. (2001). MERLOT: A faculty-focused Web site of educational resources. *Behavior Research Methods, Instruments, & Computers, 33*(2), 247–276.

Martin, F., & Ertzberger, J. (2013). Here and now mobile learning: An experimental study on the use of mobile technology. *Computers & Education, 68*, 76–85.

Matejka, K., & Kurke, L. B. (1994). Designing a great syllabus. *College Teaching, 42*, 115–117.

Mayer, R. E. (2005). Introduction to multimedia learning. In R. E. Mayer (Ed.), *The Cambridge handbook of multimedia learning* (pp. 1–24). New York: Cambridge University Press.

Mayer, R. E. (2008). Applying the science of learning: Evidence-based principles for the design of multimedia instruction. *American Psychologist, 63*(8), 760–769.

McGee, P., & Reis, A. (2012). Blended course design: A synthesis of best practices. *Journal of Asynchronous Learning Networks, 16*(4), 7–22.

McNabb, L., & Olmstead, A. (2009). Communities of integrity in online courses: Faculty member beliefs and strategies. *MERLOT Journal of Online Learning and Teaching, 5*(2), 208–221.

McNamara, J. M., Swalm, R. L., Stearne, D. J., & Covassin, T. M. (2008). Online weight training. *Journal of Strength and Conditioning Research, 22*(4), 1164–1168.

McTighe, J., & Wiggins, G. (2004). *Understanding by design: Professional development workbook.* Alexandria, VA: Association for Supervision and Curriculum Development.

Meyer, K. A. (2003). Face-to-face versus threaded discussions: The role of time and higher-order thinking. *JALN, 7*(3), 55–65.

Michael, J. (2006). Where's the evidence that active learning works? *Advances in Physiology Education, 30*, 159–167.

Michaelsen, L. K., Davidson, N., & Major, C. H. (2014). Team-based learning practices and principles in comparison with cooperative learning and problem-based learning. *Journal on Excellence in College Teaching, 25*(3–4), 57–84.

Millis, B. (1989). Helping to make connections: Emphasizing the role of the syllabus. *To Improve the Academy, 8,* 235–244.

Millis, B. (2012). *Active learning strategies in face-to-face courses.* IDEA Paper no. 53. Manhattan, KS: The IDEA Center.

Moore, J. C., & Fetzner, M. J. (2009). The road to retention: A closer look at institutions that achieve high course completion rates. *Journal of Asynchronous Learning Networks, 3*(3), 3–22.

Moore, N., & Gilmartin, M. (2010). Teaching for better learning: A blended learning pilot project with first-year geography undergraduates. *Journal of Geography in Higher Education, 34*(3), 327–344.

Moten, J., Fitterer, A., Brazier, E., Leonard, J., & Brown, A. (2013). Examining online college cyber cheating methods and prevention measures. *The Electronic Journal of e-Learning, 11*(2), 139–146.

Nguyen, L., Barton, S. M., & Nguyen, L. T. (2015). iPads in higher education—hype and hope. *British Journal of Educational Technology, 46*(1), 190–203.

Nilson, L. B. (2010). *Teaching at its best: A research-based resource for college instructors.* San Francisco, CA: Jossey-Bass.

North Virginia Community College Technology Applications Center. (2011, December 14). *Hybrid course review checklist.* Retrieved from https://www.nvcc.edu/hybrid/_docs/hybridchecklist.pdf.

O'Brien, L., Campbell, A., & Earp, S. (2005). CMS implementation as a catalyst for curricular change. In P. McGee, C. Carmean, & A. Jafari (Eds.), *Course management systems for learning* (pp. 114–130). Hershey, PA: Information Science Publishing.

Odell, M., Abbitt, J., Amos, D., & Davis, J. (1999). Developing online courses: A comparison of web-based instruction with traditional instruction. In J. Price et al. (Eds.), *Proceedings of Society for Information Technology & Teacher Education International Conference 1999* (pp. 126–130). Chesapeake, VA: Association for the Advancement of Computing in Education (AACE).

Paas, F., & Sweller, J. (2005). Implications of cognitive load theory for multimedia learning. In R. E. Mayer (Ed.), *The Cambridge handbook of multimedia learning* (pp. 27–42). New York: Cambridge University Press.

Palloff, R. M., & Pratt, K. (2007). *Building online learning communities: Effective strategies for the virtual classroom.* San Francisco, CA: Jossey-Bass.

Palloff, R. M., & Pratt, K. (2009). *Assessing the online learner: Resources and strategies for faculty.* San Francisco, CA: Jossey-Bass.

Palmer, M. S., Bach, D. J., & Streifer, A. C. (2014). Measuring the promise: A learning-focused syllabus rubric. *To Improve the Academy, 33*(1), 14–36.

Parkes, J., & Harris, M. B. (2002). The purpose of a syllabus. *College Teaching, 50*(2), 55–61.

Parry, M. (2011, August 28). Online venture energizes vulnerable college. *Chronicle of Higher Education.* Retrieved from http://chronicle.com/article/How-Big-Can-E-Learning-Get-At/128809/.

Pegrum, M., Bartle, E., & Longnecker, N. (2015). Can creative podcasting promote deep learning? The use of podcasting for learning content in an undergraduate science unit. *British Journal of Educational Technology, 46*(1), 142–152.

Peluso, D. C. C. (2012). The face-paced iPad revolution: Can educators stay up to date and relevant about these ubiquitous devices? *British Journal of Educational Technology, 43*(4), 125–127.

Picciano, A. G. (2007). Introduction. In A. G. Picciano & C. D. Dziuban (Eds.), *Blended learning, research perspectives* (pp. 5–18). Needham, MA: Sloan Consortium.

Picciano, A. G. (2009). Blending with purpose: The multimodal model. *Journal of Asynchronous Learning Networks, 13*(1), 7–18.

Picciano, A. G., & Dziuban, C. D. (Eds.). (2007). *Blended learning, research perspectives*. Needham, MA: Sloan Consortium.

Picciano, A. G., Dziuban, C. D., & Graham, C. R. (Eds.). (2014). *Blended learning, research perspectives* (Vol. 2). New York: Routledge.

Pillay, H., Irving, K., & Tones, M. (2007). Validation of the diagnostic tool for assessing tertiary students' readiness for online learning. *Higher Education Research & Development, 26*(2), 217–234.

Prince, M. (2004). Does active learning work? A review of the research. *Journal of Engineering Education, 93*(3). Retrieved from http://www4.ncsu.edu/unity/lockers/users/f/felder/public/Papers/Prince_AL.pdf

Quality Matters. (2015). *Quality Matters rubric standards*. Retrieved from https://www.qmprogram.org/qmresources/research/

Quality Matters. (2016). *Underlying principles of Quality Matters*. Retrieved from https://www.qualitymatters.org/research-grants/fipse/principles.

Reaburn, P., Muldoon, N., & Bookallil, C. (2009). Blended spaces, work based learning, and constructive alignment: Impacts on student engagement. In *Same places, different spaces. Proceedings ASCILITE Auckland 2009*. Retrieved from http://www.ascilite.org.au/conferences/auckland09/procs/raeburn.pdf.

Reasons, S. G., Valadares, K., & Slavkin, M. (2005). Questioning the hybrid model: Student outcomes in different course formats. *Journal of Asynchronous Learning Networks, 9*(1), 83–94.

Richardson, J. C., & Swan, K. (2003). Examining social presence in online courses in relation to students' perceived learning and satisfaction. *Journal of Asynchronous Learning Networks, 7*(1), 68–88.

Riffell, S., & Sibley, D. (2005). Using web-based instruction to improve large undergraduate biology courses: An evaluation of a hybrid course format. *Computers & Education, 44*(3), 217–235.

Rossing, J. P., Miller, W. M., Cecil, A. K., & Stamper, S. E. (2012). iLearning: The future of higher education? Student perceptions on learning with mobile tablets. *Journal of the Scholarship of Teaching and Learning, 12*(2), 1–26.

Rovai, A. P. (2002). Sense of community, perceived cognitive learning, and persistence in asynchronous learning networks. *The Internet and Higher Education, 5*(4), 319–332.

Saville, B. K., Zinn, T. E., Brown, A. R., & Marchuk, K. A. (2010). Syllabus detail and students' perceptions of teacher effectiveness. *Teaching of Psychology, 37*, 186–189.

Scoville, S. A., & Buskirk, T. D. (2007). Traditional and virtual microscopy compared experimentally in a classroom setting. *Clinical Anatomy, 20*(5), 565–570.

Shea, P. (2006). A study of students' sense of learning community in online environments. *Journal of Asynchronous Learning Networks, 10*(1), 35–44.

Shea, P. (2007). Towards a conceptual framework for learning in blended environments. In A. G. Picciano & C. D. Dziuban (Eds.), *Blended learning, research perspectives* (pp. 19–35). Needham, MA: Sloan Consortium.

Shuler, P., Hutchins, G., & LaShell, B. (2010). Student perceptions of tablet computers in a cooperative learning environment. *NACTA Journal, 54*(2), 11–17.

Slattery, J. M., & Carlson. J. F. (2005). Preparing an effective syllabus: Current best practices. *College Teaching, 53*(4), 159–164.

Smith, M., & Casserly, C. M. (2006). The promise of open educational resources. *Change, September/October,* 8–17.

Smith, M. F., & Razzouk, N. Y. (1993). Improving classroom communication: The case of the course syllabus. *Journal of Education for Business, 68*(4), 215–221.

Snart, J. (2010). *Hybrid learning: The perils and promise of blending online and face-to-face instruction in higher education.* Santa Barbara, CA: Praeger.

So, H. J., & Brush, T. A. (2008). Student perceptions of collaborative learning, social presence and satisfaction in a blended learning environment: Relationships and critical factors. *Computers & Education, 51*(1), 318–336.

Starenko, M., Vignare, K., & Humbert, J. (2007). Enhancing student interaction and sustaining faculty instructional innovations through blended learning. In A. G. Picciano & C. D. Dziuban (Eds.), *Blended learning, research perspectives* (pp. 161–176). Needham, MA: Sloan Consortium.

Stein, J., & Graham, C. R. (2014). *Essentials for blended learning: A standards-based guide.* New York: Routledge.

Stevens, D. D., & Cooper, J. E. (2009). *Journal keeping: How to use reflective writing for learning, teaching, professional insight and positive change.* Sterling, VA: Stylus.

Stevens, D. D., & Levi, A. J. (2005). *Introduction to rubrics: An assessment tool to save grading time, convey effective feedback, and promote student learning.* Sterling, VA: Stylus.

Sulik, G., & Keys, J. (2014). "Many students really do not yet know how to behave!": The syllabus as a tool for socialization. *Teaching Sociology, 42*(2), 151–160.

Suskie, L. (2009). *Assessing student learning: A common sense guide.* San Francisco, CA: Jossey-Bass.

Svinicki, M. D. (2004). *Learning and motivation in the postsecondary classroom.* Bolton, MA: Anker Publishing.

Tess, P. A. (2013). The role of social media in higher education classes (real and virtual)—a literature review. *Computers in Human Behavior, 29*(5), A60–A68.

Thompson, B. (2007). The syllabus as a communication document: Constructing and presenting the syllabus. *Communication Education, 56,* 54–71.

Tu, C. H. (2001). How Chinese perceive social presence: An examination of interaction in online learning environment. *Educational Media International, 38*(1), 45–60.

Tynan, B., Ryan, Y., & Lamont-Mills, A. (2015). Examining workload models in online and blended teaching. *British Journal of Educational Technology, 46*(1), 5–15.

U.S. Department of Education, Office of Planning, Evaluation, and Policy Development. (2010). *Evaluation of evidence-based practices in online learning: A meta-analysis and review of online learning studies.* Washington, DC: Government Printing Office.

Varvel, V. E., Jr. (2005). Honesty in education. In *Pointers & clickers, ION's technology tip of the month.* Retrieved from http://www.ion.uillinois.edu/resources/pointers clickers/2005_01/VarvelCheatPoint2005.pdf.

Vovides, Y., Sanchez-Alonso, S., Mitropoulou, V., & Nickmans, G. (2007). The use of e-learning course management systems to support learning strategies and to improve self-regulated learning. *Educational Research Review, 2,* 64–74.

Wakefield, J., & Smith, D. (2012). From Socrates to satellites: iPad learning in an undergraduate course. *Creative Education 3*(5), 643–648.

Walvoord, B. E., & Anderson, V. J. (2010). *Effective grading: A tool for learning and assessment in college (2nd ed.).* San Francisco, CA: Jossey-Bass.

Wasley, P. (2008). The syllabus becomes a repository of legalese. *Chronicle of Higher Education.* Retrieved from http://crmtview.asc.ohio-state.edu/currofc/docs/committee/406/Syllabus_TheChronicle.pdf.

Watts, D. (2014). Lessons learned from the Facebook study. *Chronicle of Higher Education.* Retrieved from http://chronicle.com/blogs/conversation/2014/07/09/lessons-learned-from-the-facebook-study/.

Wesp, R., Kash, M., Sandry, J., & Patton, L. (2013). Should syllabi communicate expectations regarding appropriate classroom behaviors? *Syllabus, 2*(2), 1–10.

Wiggins, G., & McTighe, J. (2005). *Understanding by design.* Alexandria, VA: Association for Supervision & Curriculum Development.

Wiley, D., Bliss, T. J., & McEwen, M. (2014). Open educational resources: A review of the literature. In J. M. Spector (Ed.), *Handbook of research on educational communication and technology* (pp. 781–789). New York: Springer.

Wodzicki, K., Schwämmlein, E., & Moskaliuk, J. (2012). "Actually, I wanted to learn": Study-related knowledge exchange on social networking sites. *The Internet and Higher Education, 15(1),* 9–14.

Wolfman-Arent, A. (2014). Why this professor is encouraging Facebook use in his classroom. *Chronicle of Higher Education.* Retrieved from http://chronicle.com/blogs/wiredcampus/why-this-professor-is-encouraging-facebook-use-in-his-classroom/54223.

ABOUT THE CONTRIBUTORS

Kathryn (Katie) E. Linder is the research director for Ecampus at Oregon State University, where she helps make research actionable through the creation of evidence-based resources related to effective online teaching, learning, and program administration. Formerly, she directed the Center for Teaching and Scholarly Excellence at Suffolk University in Boston. Katie is the author of *Rampage Violence Narratives* (Lexington Books, 2014) and the host of the "Research in Action" podcast. Some of her more recent journal publications can be found in *Innovative Higher Education* and the *Journal of Open, Distance, and e-Learning*. Katie earned her BA in English literature and creative writing from Whitworth University and her MA and PhD in women's studies from The Ohio State University.

Linda Bruenjes is the associate director of technology innovation in learning and teaching for the Center for Teaching and Scholarly Excellence at Suffolk University, where she supports faculty in the design and assessment of online and technology-enhanced course design. Previously, she was the director for Academic Computing and Online Learning at Lasell College, where she developed and delivered the college's online faculty certification program. Linda is the coauthor of the "Internet2" chapter in the *Handbook of Computer Networks* (Wiley, 2007) and the *Internet Encyclopedia* (Wiley, 2004). She received her EdD in Leadership in Schooling from the University of Massachusetts Lowell.

Danny Fontaine is the director of the First Year Experience Project at the University of Cape Town (UCT), South Africa. As director, she is responsible for providing strategic direction and oversight to the university's programming—both centralized and faculty-specific—for first-year students. She is also involved with various research initiatives of the newly-founded South African National Resource Centre for First Year Students and Students in Transition—particularly research that focuses on student success during their first year in higher education. Prior to her current position, she was the assistant director for the Centre for Teaching and Scholarly Excellence at Suffolk University in Boston. Danielle completed her BS, honors, and MA in environmental and geographical science at UCT; she completed her PhD in urban geography at Clark University in Worcester, Massachusetts.

Sarah Smith is the program manager for blended learning at Babson Executive and Enterprise Education and performs as a teaching and learning architect with a focus on delivering first-class and effective experiences in a scalable, repeatable manner to global clients. Smith has over 12 years of experience in developing and implementing a wide array of instructional technology training and professional development opportunities for faculty at all levels of expertise, focused on facilitating student learning and integrating technology with curriculum. She has designed and implemented several multiday blended and online course design institutes that train faculty on the fundamentals of blended teaching and learning and has presented internationally on designing training methods for faculty to transition traditional courses to blended and online models. Smith holds a BA in graphic/information design from Central Connecticut State University, an MS in education technology from Central Connecticut State University, and a MBA from Curry College.

Victoria Wallace has over 18 years of instructional design experience in the financial, technical, and academic fields. As part of the Massachusetts General Hospital (MGH) Institute of Health Professions Office of the Provost team, Victoria works with faculty and staff providing instructional support in the design, development, facilitation, and evaluation of course materials to improve teaching strategies and the student experience. She consults with faculty integrating research-based principles, best practices, and the latest technologies into course curriculum. Prior to her role at MGH IHP, Victoria worked in Northeastern University's Educational Technology Center supporting faculty designing and developing online courses and promoting and managing outreach and pilot programs. She also taught online in the instructional design graduate program at University of Massachusetts-Boston. Victoria holds a BA in psychology from University of Central Florida; a MEd in instructional design from University of Massachusetts-Boston; and is currently pursuing her EdD in curriculum, teaching, learning, and leadership at Northeastern University.

INDEX